# Prophetic Training

## A Guidebook for the Prophet and Ministers in the Prophetic Ministry

Adetokunbo Obasa



ISBN: 1544172214
ISBN-13: 978-1544172217

# DEDICATION

To my wonderful wife Katherine and my sons Joshua and Josiah. They have been such a blessing to me.

# CONTENTS

# ACKNOWLEDGMENTS

I want to give thanks to God Almighty for His mercies and His blessings. My Sustainer, My Defender, My Helper, the One who has been so merciful to me. My appreciation goes to all the members of House of David (A Covenant Church), for their support and encouragement. My prayer is that the Lord will reward all your labors of love in Jesus Name. Amen.

My sincere appreciation goes to all my friends in the Ministry, men and women of God that the Lord has used to encourage us in obeying the Lord in the assignment He gave to us, may He send divine helpers to support your vision in Jesus Name. Amen.

I want to thank especially my covenant daughter, Julienne King for helping me. The Lord will bless you in Jesus Name. Amen.

I want to thank God for my Sweetheart, whom the Lord has used tremendously in my personal life and ministry. I cannot thank her enough, only God can reward her for all her labors in Jesus Name. Amen. The boys, I love them so much. My Father in Heaven who gave them to us will watch over them in Jesus Name. Amen.

# *Prophetic Training*

# CHAPTER 1

# WHAT IS A PROPHET

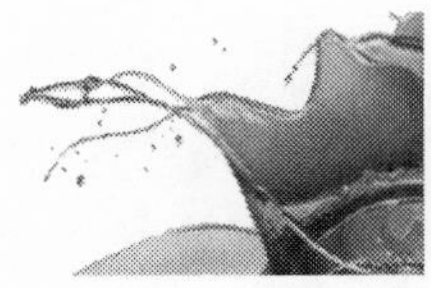

We are going to look at Prophetic School of Ministry. We are going to be looking at some areas whereby one can understand what a prophetic ministry is. Today, we quickly are going to look over what a prophet is because if you don't know what a prophet is, then you cannot even understand what a prophetic ministry is. So who is a prophet? A prophet is a person who speaks by divine inspiration or as the interpreter through whom the will of God is expressed. That is one level of definition. Another level of definition is a person gifted with profound moral insight and exceptional powers of expression.

Anyone that is gifted with profound moral insight, he sees more than what everybody else sees. He hears more than what everybody hears. That type of person can also be referred to as a prophet. A prophet is also somebody that is called a soothsayer. Most of the time in the Bible, they refer to them as a "soothsayer" or a seer- somebody that sees. Somebody that hears. Amen.

Another definition of a prophet is somebody that is a chief spokesman of a movement or a cause. Somebody that is a chief spokesman is somebody that leads a group of people and most of the time it is usually spiritually inclined. It is usually a spiritual, religious background of a group of people – a deliverer for a purpose. Somebody that fights a cause. That's why sometimes they refer to MLK as a prophet. He's not really a prophet, but he was leading a cause. He was leading a movement.

So, a prophet can also be called that. A prophet is also a person that predicts the future. A person that God gives insight about the future is also a prophet. Someone who claims to discover divine hidden knowledge with the aid of spiritual power is also a prophet. Somebody that claims to have a hidden grace or spiritual power to discover hidden knowledge, knowledge that is hidden from everybody else; he can declare it and he knows about it, he has answers to those things. We see an example of that in the Bible; somebody like Moses. Moses was telling the people what the Lord was saying though they did not see it. He was telling them what God has already said to him. He has a hidden knowledge. He has knowledge of something that everybody else does not have, and he is doing that with the aid of spiritual powers.

We saw the power displayed of Moses when he put his hand in his dress and his hand became leprous. He put his hand back into his dress and brought it out again and his hand became clean. Anybody that displays that kind of power can also be referred to as prophet because he has some hidden power. He's not operating with ordinary power. He's operating with a spiritual power with the backing of a Divine being to do certain things that everybody else cannot do.

We can also call a prophet an interpreter of the will of God. Somebody that interprets the will of God and somehow they have a knowledge of what the will of God is. Somebody of that status can also be referred to as prophet. We talk of Jonah. Jonah did not do anything extraordinary or outstanding, but Jonah told a whole nation that God said "you are a sinner". The will of God was being declared over a nation. "You are all a sinner. If you don't repent,

God will destroy all of you." So, somebody like that can also be called a prophet. Somebody that interprets the will of God, the purpose of God- the agenda of God. Praise the Lord.

So, what are the signs of a prophetic ministry? You cannot say you are a prophet without having some signs. You will begin to feel uncomfortable in some certain areas or experience some things that you will know that you are tending towards that ministry. I want to quickly look at some points that if this is the reason you want to become a prophet, then you are in the wrong ministry. Number one, if the reason you want to be a prophet is for glamour, then you have made a big mistake. Prophetic ministry is not for glamour. By the time we go through some details of these teachings, I pray that none of you will change your mind. Amen. (I didn't know that this is what a prophetic ministry is). I hope that's not what you will say. In Jesus Name. Amen.

Prophetic ministry, your life becomes a sign to the people you are leading especially when you are called into the kind of prophetic ministry that people like Ezekiel, Jeremiah, and Isaiah was called. Your life represents what God is trying to do or say to the people. So, it's not an easy thing to be called into this type of prophetic ministry. So, if your reason of coming into the prophetic is because of glamour, then this type of prophetic ministry will not work for you.

Secondly, if the reason why you want to be a prophet is because of recognition, then you are also in the wrong place. Prophets are seldom recognized or placed on a very high level. Look at the story in the 1 Kings and 2 Kings, the only time they call for a prophet is when they are in trouble. You don't hear about prophets eating in the king's palace or prophet walking with the king or riding on horses. Nobody knows them or are interested in their lives. The only time they are interested in them is when there is war and they want to know the agenda and the mind of God concerning the war or a particular situation that is confusing to them. They do not talk to them every day. You are not recognized. You don't live a life of recognition. You are not placed on as a high pedestal of the city where everybody comes and bow down to you, no. It's only the king. Some of the wise kings, not even all of the kings, in the books of 1 and 2 Kings will begin to realize that when they run into trouble, they will tell everyone around them, "can we find a prophet?" because they know that when they find a prophet, they have answers.

So if your reason of being in the prophetic is for people to bow down to you, you are in the wrong ministry. Most of the time, nobody wants to even talk to you especially when God has given you a prophetic ministry to just pinpoint trouble. Some of the prophets in the Bible, their assignment that God gave them is to just pin point trouble. People will not like you for that. They don't want to hear your voice. Amen. Can you imagine a prophet went to somebody's house and says "prepare your house, you are about to die". "I'm sick, tell me something good." Then the prophet says, "Prepare your house. You are about to die". Amen.

The prophet delivered that message without fear. He delivered and walked out without any emotions. How can you just pronounce a death sentence on somebody like that without any feelings and walked out without a good bye. God didn't tell him to pray for the sick man. NO prayer, no deliverance. He left. While he was going, the other one that the message was delivered to begins to pray. And God said, I'll change my mind. God says, "Hey, my instrument! I've forgiven that one. Go back and tell him good news." That is a prophet. That is the work of a prophet. So, if you are looking for recognition, you cannot get it. You won't get it.

You do exactly what God tells you without adding or subtracting anything.

If the reason you are in the prophetic ministry is for self-exaltation, "I have arrived", "this is me", you will not get that either. You are in the wrong ministry, because most of the time there is no place in the society for a prophet. As a matter of fact, even Jesus Christ, our Lord and Savior went through persecution of a prophetic ministry. He said, "a prophet is without honor even in his own house". People that He grew up with did not believe in Him. He had to take the headquarters of His ministry to the Gentiles. He did not settle down in Nazareth because they did not recognize Him there. They didn't believe in Him and that's why if you are looking for exaltation, nobody will exalt you. Fortunately for Jesus Christ, He did not focus only on the prophetic ministry, He focused more on the Shepherd ministry and a deliverance ministry. So that makes Him popular among the believers, among the ones that are hungry for miracles, etc.

So, Jesus Christ combined all those offices together. So, that's what makes the difference of the ministry of Jesus Christ. Even though, He was rejected by His people because of His prophetic anointing, He was accepted in some other places because He was also a deliverance minister. He was also a preacher of the Word. He was also a blessing to the people. Praise the LORD!

So, again if you are looking for self-exaltation, nobody will give you that platform because of the kind of anointing you carry that makes you walk differently. Amen.

As a prophet, if you want to always be right, then you are in the wrong ministry. These 4 categories of things that I have mentioned are very, very important to us. You must settle that in your spirit. You can't always be right. You are going to be wrong, and wrong, and wrong, and the reason for that is because God is trying to prepare you for a call that has to do with death. I told us that it is a call to death not to glory. Especially those of us that are trying to serve God in this capacity, He must prepare your mind, spirit, body, and flesh. This call is a call to death and we must settle that in our spirit, people of God. Amen. We must die to the flesh.

So, how do you know that you have a prophetic anointing over your life? How do you have an idea? How do you feel? One of the main things that I want you to take note of is that you must be a failure.

1. You must be a failure totally. You have tried every other thing, it has not worked. You have put everything together. You have put all your smartness, your wisdom, everything that you know how to do, it has not worked. You have resigned yourself and said without God, I am a failure. You have resigned yourself that it is only in God that I can be anything. If you don't see yourself as a failure, then you cannot be a prophet. That's number one.

2. You cannot trust yourself. Of course you can't trust yourself because you have failed and failed and failed and you have gotten to a point that even when your mind is telling you to do something, you don't trust your mind. "No, I've tried that before and it didn't work." "Don't disappoint me again, I'd rather wait on God." "I'd rather depend on Him." "If He tells me to wait here for 3 years, then that's what I will do." In fact, people of God, you have gotten to a point that you discover that one day of favor with God is better than 2,000 years of suffering. So, you want to wait on the Lord. You prefer to wait and not do anything on your own anymore. So, you cannot trust yourself because of your past

experiences.

3. You are not sure where you are going. Whether you are going in the right direction. That's a good sign that you have a prophetic anointing because everything that God will be telling you to do, you are not even sure if anybody will listen to you. They will ask if you are okay or are you crazy or mad because what you are going to be hearing will not make sense. It's a spiritual walk and that's why it has to be because you are not sure of yourself. If you are sure of yourself then you are not ready for that ministry. You cannot be sure of yourself because you are an instrument. This is a sign that you are in a prophetic ministry. You are looking at yourself and asking "why is this happening to me, O'God?"

You can't tell anybody. They won't understand you. You are taking steps to just make you feel better. You fast for yourself. You will deliver yourself. Pray on top of your head. All this you do just to make your life a little bit better. You are just not sure of yourself, but that is a good feeling and a sign that you are in a prophetic ministry. Amen.

The signs that are very, very visible are the following:

1. A burning desire within, for the body of Christ to assist and to warn people about their daily walk with the Lord. This thing will take hold of you. It will be a heavy burden in your spirit. It bothers you when you see Christians that are not disciplined. It bothers you when you see people walking in ignorance. You ask yourself, "When are these people going to change?" It takes hold of you. You want to warn them. God has made me to do certain things that I don't really want to do. It wasn't easy for me to do those things. The result was not good. You have no control of yourself. You just want to help somebody. It takes hold of you totally. It consumes you.

2. People will not share your passion. They will tell you, "Don't rock the boat." "Calm down." "Are you Jesus?" "Giving, giving. Sow, sow, sow. Pray, pray, pray. Read Bible, read Bible. What is it?" "Why are you studying so much?" It's because there is a burning desire. Most of the time, if that burning desire is not controlled, that's why you will see some people that will just go and start a church.

Now, a burning desire does not mean you should just go and start a church. Looking at a church at this point. It's so beautiful, but you don't know what is behind what you are seeing. There's a lot of things happening in the background. People just see us sitting down here and they don't even know what has happened in the spiritual realm.

There's a lot happening in the spiritual. Can you imagine?, if God had not been merciful to me. Look at that fire that just burned my car. For it to be physical like that, do you know what the enemy really intended? That means that the intention was for us to perish totally. Now, can you imagine if the neighbor had not seen the fire, we would have died. You see God has a way of doing things to protect His own with jealousy. Somebody has to see that fire. Somebody had to wake us up.

As much as they hated Joseph, somebody has to say, "we are not shedding blood". "I don't care how much you hate him, me too, I hate him, we are not killing him." God will put somebody in the midst of that situation or in that circumstance that will protect the life and the soul of that person. That's what He does. So, you just don't jump into things, if you do, you are not covered. You are not protected. Do you know how many churches have started and have closed? You just don't start these things. If God did not call you to do it, you are not covered. You are not protected. It's just like insurance, if flood happens. If your insurance does not cover floods, you are on your own. Same thing. If it's not your calling and you step into it, you're on your own.

Secondly, if you're supposed to be trained and you didn't allow the process of training to be completed, you're on your own. Can you imagine, if a drop-out student, is not useful to the society, can't get a job. He has half knowledge. He's not complete. They will be talking about Physics and since he dropped out, he wouldn't know the answer because he dropped out. So, he's like a plague to the society. He's like a cancer. He started but he didn't finish. So he cannot talk boldly about science and yet he cannot get a job. Terrible position to be. So, your passion to be a prophet has to be channeled in the right way to be used of God.

For example, let's look at what happened to the sons of Aaron. They went and mixed strange fire before the Lord. God did not even explain to them what they did was wrong. God just killed them, straight away. They were punished because their father has commanded them the way they ought to do the assignment that was given. Their father has been commanded, "tell your sons, even though they have a desire to do my business, they have to do it lawfully". And when they make mistake, God in the Old Testament, did not explain to them what they did was wrong, He just killed them. Two boys in a day. So we have to understand the sensitivity of this assignment. Your desire is order oriented and it is not about yourself. You will have desire for other people. Your focus is not on yourself. You can give your last to people.

Money is not important to a prophet. What does he want to do with money?! Money cannot get him/her anywhere because money is another god. So, you are people oriented because God will take care of you, if you are a true prophet. You can never lack.

You can never be stranded. To tell you the truth, people of God, I don't know how this situation will end. The situation about the fire happened on March 1st, I didn't know what would happen. I didn't know how God will restore us. I didn't have a vision of it.

As a prophet, God will never leave you stranded. So, if you are trying to help yourself, you cannot be a successful prophet. Your passion is for others. Your joy is to be concerned about other people. Other people is what is driving you. You are just thinking about other people. How can I help? How can I bless this one? What can I do to help? What can I do to help the church? How can I pray for this?

4. You must be prepared to pay a price. As a prophet, if you are not willing to pay a price then you cannot be a successful prophet. Prophetic anointing is very, very sensitive. You are declaring thus says the Lord. God wants to be sure you are hearing correctly. God wants to be sure that you are trained to say the truth, because as we study on, you will see the judgement of God on false prophets. We are going to study that because you need to know.

So, if you are a true prophet, you have to be trained. If you are not trained, you cannot operate successfully under that anointing. It is very dangerous. So, you must be prepared to pay a price before you enter into it. If you desire it sincerely, you will go through that pain of servanthood, and I read Matthew 20:26, "…whoever wants to become great among you must be your servant". You must have a servant's heart. You love to minister to other people's need. When you don't do it, you feel bad. You cannot hear that something is going wrong in somebody else's life. You throw yourself into it. That is prophetic anointing.

Prophetic anointing cannot be borrowed. It's like what

happened in 2 Kings chapter 6 verse 1-7, "Master, master, my axe's head fell into the water." He didn't say, "well, let's go and buy another one." No, because some people will not accept that as their axe's head. Axe head in that olden times, is personal to people. They have their shapes and the way they shaped their own personal axes. So, if you borrow from somebody and you lose that axe head and if you buy another one, it will not look like the one that you borrowed.

So, the man of God said, "well, I know that this is very, very important." It's just like an anointing. You cannot borrow an anointing. If it's personal to you, it's personal to you. You can't borrow it. That's why you see the seven sons of Sceva, "in the name of Jesus that Paul preached, come out!" And the demons said, "you are borrowing anointing." "What are you talking about? We know Jesus. We know Paul, but who are you?" And the Bible says they came out and they dealt with those people. Tore them up. That's why it's not good to borrow anointing. Don't borrow anointing.

If you are not walking in it yourself, don't try to be what you are not. It's very dangerous. For example, the kind of prayers we pray in this church, can you imagine if God is not on our side. You are dead. You are dead meat. Why, it's good to pray those prayers, Jesus Christ said, since the day of John the Baptist, the Kingdom of God suffereth violently and only the violent taketh by force.

If you say I won't pray against the devil, the devil will come after you. For example, Jesus Christ was teaching the disciples how to pray, one of the things He said in that prayer was, "deliver us from evil". Why would He put it there if there is no evil? That means Jesus also recognizes that there is evil. So, we must understand that you do not be a defensive Christian only. You must also be on the offensive and we need God to deliver us from those forces of darkness. Amen.

Hunger to pray for others. It's very, very important to the ministry of the prophetic. You must love to intercede and pray for others. Prophetic anointing changes the atmosphere. When you have a prophetic anointing, you get into a place and everybody is affected by your presence. If you have this prophetic calling on your life, your preparation will take a long time. It is a difficult and troublesome process. You are broken, battered, and subdued before the Lord can use you.

I have heard people tell me, God does not force people to do things. Well, if you are not important to His Kingdom, He does not have to force you. He doesn't need you, but the people that He needs, the people that are ordained for His purpose, He will break them down. Amen. If you are not important, He won't worry about you. You can do whatever you like, He doesn't care. But, if He's interested in your life, He will break you down, especially when you have an assignment in the Kingdom you must fulfill.

God doesn't play. Remember, if He does that to His own personal Son, what will He do to you? He didn't have mercy on Jesus Christ. Do you know how difficult it is to be under a father that is not an anointed father, that doesn't know anything about the Kingdom? That his job is a carpenter. Do you know how difficult that is? And here you are, the Creator of Heaven and Earth. You know everything and look at your earthly father, he doesn't know nothing. And, he's telling you to go and put the chair together and file the wood. "Put the nail here." "Sit down here. Stand up there". I know Jesus will be looking like "God, You really made me to suffer?" "Who is he talking to?"

He had to go through that for 30 years. It's not a joke. 30

years and you cannot do any unnecessary moves. You are not supposed to disrespect him. You are not supposed to disrespect your mommy. You have to be like a normal child. Did they record any miracle about Jesus Christ for all those years? Nothing, except the only time when He went out of the way in Luke chapter 2, and the Bible says in verse 51, "He went back home and He became subjected unto them". We did not hear anything again from Him for 18 years. Do you know how difficult that is? Wow! That is more than going to the cross. At least you die within one day right? They nail you to the cross and you die one day, but 30 years under that man. And you cannot do anything other than what you are instructed. That is painful.

And that is where the prophetic anointing becomes very interesting because God will squeeze you. Look at what God did with David. You know David combined the anointing of a prophet, a King, and a priest. He has the combination of the 3 anointings. That's why David could write the things that he wrote. That's why he could talk about the death of Jesus Christ in the book of Psalms. That's why he could talk about Judas in the book of Psalms because he has a prophetic anointing to see some things. That's why he can say in the book of Psalm chapter 51, "don't take Your Holy Spirit from me". Holy Spirit was not recorded in the Old Testament by anybody. It was David that introduced the importance of the Holy Spirit in the life of a child of God. He said don't take Your Holy Spirit from me because when You take it, I'm finished. That is a prophetic anointing. Look at his writings in the book of Psalms.

Here we are Jesus has not even come to tell us how important the Comforter will be to us, and here David is talking about it in the book of Psalms already.

So you can understand the kind of grace, but David suffered for that kind of anointing. You know that right? Suffered very well. He was anointed at the age of 17 and did not become a king until the age of 30. He had to run for his dear life. Had to run from pillar to post. He had to be like a madman at one time in the land of Philistines, with spit drooling in his mouth so they wouldn't kill him. That is training. Seeing your enemy so close and you cannot fight, but to seek help.

God also trained David by giving him opportunity to kill Saul. This opportunity was presented to him twice, but look at what was in his heart, "how can I stretch out my hand towards the Lord's anointed?' That's training. This is the person that you have been running from that has made your life terrible, from pillar to post. Now, you have the opportunity to finish your enemy and you can't do it.

So if you have been under intense pressure, problem, failure, and persecution, this will be a sign of a prophetic anointing. It's a call to death. You. Must. Die. Amen.

I have some questions to ask. When you look at the church in its current condition, how do you feel? How would you consider your approach to ministry? How do you consider your Christian walk so far? What has been your experience as you sought God for your call? Do you receive revelation? What kind of person do you say you are? How would you rate your prayer life on a scale? Do you hear constantly and clearly from the Holy Spirit? Are you indebted to the Word of God? Can you identify your flesh? Amen.

Name the major prophets and the minor prophets. When anybody ask you to mention major prophets, they are talking about the books. Amen. We have examples of prophets. If they ask you, Name the prophets of the Bible, it's totally different than when they are asking you to name the minor prophet and the major prophet.

If they say name the prophets, of course you can name Moses, Elijah, all those individuals, but when they say name the major prophets and the minor prophets, they are referring to those that wrote books in the Bible. Don't forget that.

How many hours of prayer did you pray for the whole week? How much time for your personal Bible study in a day? Praise the Lord. Read Romans 12:13-14 for more of an introduction to the prophetic anointing. Some key areas to look at are intercession, prayer, and love. These things will help on the journey. Amen.

# CHAPTER 2

# PREPARATION FOR THE PROPHETIC OFFICE

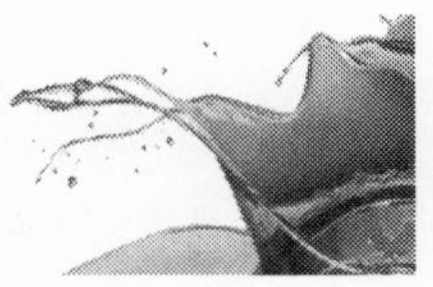

The office of the prophetic is speaking the Word of God. Because it is the Word of God, it is not your job to be worried how it will come to pass. That is God's part to do. In the book of Isaiah 55:11, the Bible says,

***11 My Word will never come back void.***

It is His word. It is not your word. The Word of God will accomplish that which He pleases and it will prosper in which He sent it. Sometimes when you speak and it does not happen the way you spoke, don't feel bad, it's not your word. It is the Word of God. People will not accept that word sometimes. Don't feel bad if they don't. Just continue to do what you have to do. So, in preparing for the prophetic office, let's look at 2 Corinthians 4:8-11,

***8 We are troubled on every side, yet not distressed. We are perplexed, but not in despair. 9 Persecuted, but not forsaken. Cast down, but not destroyed. 10 Always bearing about in the body the dying of the Lord Jesus, that the life also of Jesus might be made manifest in our body. 11 For we which live are always delivered unto death for Jesus' sake, that the life also of Jesus might be made manifest in our mortal flesh.***

So, we are going to look at some points today that will give you the stages of your preparation. You will experience rejection.

You are going to be despised. You are going to be ostracized. This is the process by which you are prepared. You are never prepared when things are easy for you. Let's look at Isaiah 48:10, look at what the Lord says.

***[10]Behold, I have refined thee, but not with silver; I have chosen thee in the furnace of affliction.***

God's gold are always chosen in the furnace of affliction. He does not make His choices in ease. He makes His choice in the furnace of affliction. He does not make His choice on the easy road.

1. The first thing you will experience on your road of preparation is that everything goes wrong. Making you into a vessel, fit for His use, you can never be right. We are troubled on every side, and what God is trying to do by troubling you on every side is to put your emotions out of action. Your emotions must die completely. Your feelings and emotions must be killed. Until that emotion is murdered and killed, you are not ready yet. God will continue to work upon you until that part of you is dead. Until that part of you dies totally, you cannot really move forward in the anointing. Amen.

You will be doing small, small things, because God sees that you are still a baby. I'm not sure if anyone have noticed this, but when you became a born again Christian, fresh in the Kingdom, before you pray any small prayer, God answers. Before you cry, He answers. As you mature, sometimes you pray a whole year and He wouldn't listen to you or you will not hear anything from Him regarding your request. You understand? Now, when you are matured, He doesn't answer you quickly and He is not trying to please you anymore. That time is over. Now, you have to wait. Amen.

When I became born again at that time just as I mentioned above because God was still pampering me, I thought I knew how to pray better than anybody else. I would be boasting in the house thinking that I am so good, but what I didn't know was that because I was fresh in the Kingdom, things were so easy. I would say to my mom, 'mommy, let me pray for you". Mommy would be looking at me like, "what is wrong with this one". And I would say, "God answers all my prayers." She would say, "Just wait." When she was telling me that at that time, I was just thinking that she was jealous. But now, I understand.

And God will do that for you for a while. Look at children, before they cry, daddy moves. Let them be 16 years old, he's talking about a shoe for a whole month, you don't have time for him. "I don't have money". "Manage what you are wearing." Because, now he's grown. You are not going to be jumping up and down for him anymore, but a baby, every attention is on him/her. The moment the baby starts walking, the attention will reduce. That's the truth.

As he grows older, the attention will be diminishing. What makes us as children of God being blessed by God as we mature is when you walk in total obedience. That's when He begins to find pleasure in your life. Not when you are disobedient. So, He is trying to kill your emotions.

The prophet's emotions are challenged. Your mind tries to reason the Word of God out. That's why I laugh when people say they are a thinker. God will not talk to you when you think too much because you will reason out everything He is telling you. You want to find answers to everything and if you don't find the answer, you look at this church and that church and when they don't do it the way you want, you have a lot of questions because your mind is so developed and you are a thinker. I used to think too, but God has to help me. It's been 13 years. He's been training me. A lot of you don't know that. He's been training me and training everybody. If the church had grown the way God has told me it will grow, I would be incapacitated.

You know success is very dangerous. If you are successful and you don't have capacity to carry that success, you will die. That's why you see people win 1 million dollar lottery and they kill themselves by drug abuse. They don't think. They can't sit down and plan for that money. Before 2 or 3 months, they are broke. They are not thinking straight because they are not ready for the success.

That's why God does not take children with pamper to war, the pampers will fall off. He will train you. He will kill your reasoning mind. You will not be able to reason Him out. Until your mind is dead. Your mind has to be crucified. Why your mind has to die is that the instructions that He will be giving you will not make sense to the mind.

Let me give you an example. Remember the widow of Zarephath, (go and read that story very well in 1 Kings 17), I have commanded a woman to feed you there. That's what the Lord told him. When he saw that woman, he had to speak to that woman himself. The woman was not willing to do what God asked her to do. Even though God commanded the woman, God did not inform the woman about the man of God that was coming.

So, when the man of God said, "go and make me a cake first", the woman said, "this is my last bread." "We are going to make our last food and die". The man of God had to take his prophetic position to declare. If he did not declare, nothing would have happened. And you know what God is trying to do in that stage?

God was trying to humble the man of God that no matter the anointing you carry, somebody has to help you and if you don't know how to talk to them, you will not get that blessing.

So, it's very, very important that our mind is left out. That woman wanted to discourage that man of God. She wanted to him to reason with his mind. "We are about to make the last food and die." The mind will automatically tell the man of God, "you are talking to the wrong person. This person cannot help you. They are about to make their last food and die. They don't have enough." So the man of God had to declare, "as long as Lord liveth, the oil and the flour will not cease. Make me a bread first".

You have to be broken in order to obey God in those certain circumstances. If you are not broken, your mind will reason that instruction out. Your mind will say, God has commanded this woman, why is this woman resisting? The woman should be willing to give me the food. Why must I tell her? It's a lie.

Let me give you another example. God told Moses, "Command the people to give an offering." When Moses went to speak to the people, he said, "whoever is willing, let him bring an offering." As a prophet, your mind will be telling you look at these people, "stiffnecked peopled", they will never give anything. If God did not tell Moses  to do that, he would not have done it.

So, you must understand the process. Your emotions and your mind must be put out of action totally. It does not make sense to tell a servant to go and cut a stick, put it in the water and iron will float (2 Kings 6:6). That was the instruction from Heaven. It goes against every law of physics. How can a stick sink and iron begin to float. Your mind must die. If your mind is not dead, then you cannot receive that type of instruction because your mind will tell you that doesn't make sense. Stick for iron to swim? No, you didn't hear God right. Maybe God said put another iron. You understand? Your mind will want to reason the instruction out.

Have you thought about it? Jesus had the power to heal anyone, because He has done it before in other parts of the Bible. He has told lepers to be clean and they were clean, but this particular case, He told them to go and show themselves to the priest. That is the instruction from Heaven. Remember, Jesus says "I don't do anything other than what my Father is doing or whatever I see my Father do, that's what I do." So, that means that instruction to go and show themselves to the priest came directly from Heaven, but it does not make sense. How can a leper go to the church and show himself to the priest? A leper that is not supposed to be in the service talking to the priest! So, you must be able to hear and not ask questions even though the instruction does not make any sense, but it makes God.

That's why your mind must be put out of action. It doesn't make sense to follow a man with a pitcher as he enters a house in a whole city (Luke 22:10). How many men with a pitcher would be in the city? Jesus Christ did not name the man with a pitcher. He said follow the man with a pitcher. Even the people that follow that kind of instruction must be broken because they should have asked Jesus Christ, "a city?" "How many pitchers are we going to see?" "You said follow a man. Which man?" "Does he have a name?"

So, even those instructions given to Peter and John, they obeyed Jesus because they have seen Him in different dimensions. They have seen that this man is powerful. They are broken to follow that type of instruction. The instruction says, "Don't talk to him. Whichever house he enters." You understand? Those are strange things that your mind will want to reason out. If you are the one that type of instruction was given, you would never follow it. Because you will first ask God, "a man with a pitcher in a whole city?" "There are a lot of people with a pitcher on their head." "Daddy, what are you talking about?" But, you see because they have seen Him do strange things, they didn't ask questions. When they went into that city, they saw a man with a pitcher. The interesting part of it on this particular day, they saw only one man with a pitcher.

They didn't sit there and begin to argue with Him. They just followed the instruction. The Bible said that they did not miss it. They followed the right man. Your mind must be completely put out of action because you will never be able to follow those type of instructions as a prophet if your mind is still very active.

3. Prophets in training are persecuted. Persecuted but not forsaken. Emotions, mind, and will are the functions of the soul. These 3 functions of the soul must be put on hold. If you are not willing to put that part of your life on hold, you will not be able to function successfully in this ministry. You will be persecuted because everything you want to do, people will not let you do it. Persecution most of the time, it is done by people who are closest to you. Can you believe, Jesus is preaching one day and His family does not even come to church that day? Can you believe that? They didn't come to service, but they came to excuse Him out of the service. We all know what Jesus Christ said to them.

They showed up because they saw that the ministry was successful. They would not support Him, but they want to show off that they are the family of Jesus Christ. They showed up in the service. Jesus Christ is preaching and they send somebody to Him, "please can you tell Jesus Christ that somebody wants to talk to Him."

Jesus Christ says, "Me? I'm not coming. You didn't come to

church and now you want to disturb the service?" Jesus Christ says, "Who is my mother? Who is my brother?" He says that only people who are my sister, my brother, my mother are the ones doing the will of God. He did not answer them.

Some people would say, "that person has become arrogant and that's an insult." It's not. I will not tolerate even my wife to disrupt the services here. I will not allow anybody to distract me on this job. Anybody that tries it, I will embarrass the person. I don't care if they leave because that is an attack from the pit of hell. He's preaching and you have not been coming to church. Now, because the ministry is successful, you now show up.

People that know you very well will not honor you. It takes absolute humility. The Lord has been dealing with me and sometimes it's just so difficult what God is saying. I will tell the Lord, "Lord, can I pray furthermore?" And the Lord will say, "I have not changed my mind. What I told you before is what I'm still saying." It's some difficult messages and if I don't say it, it will just be churning in me. I promised the Lord, that I will deliver them. Your will must be put out of action.

So, if all of you are willing to do that, I welcome you to the prophetic ministry. These are the 3 most difficult areas to fight- your emotions, your will, and your mind. What you feel you should do. What you think you should do. God will not let you do it. Until you let those areas of your life go, you will not be a successful prophet.

Do you know that's the problem of Jonah? God had to teach him a lesson. Can you imagine a prophet whose will and emotion has not been in check? That's why God allowed that tree to grow over his head to give him a shadow for a few days, and God took away that tree to teach him a lesson. You are angry. Angry for what? Can you make anything happen? Do you have the power to make anything happen? Why are you angry with the tree I killed yesterday? Do you understand? So, God had to put his mind, his will, and his emotions out of action.

God says, "I save souls." And Jonah is angry, "I knew you were going to save them." Would you not be happy that people are saved. What is your own? That is why your emotions have to die. As a prophet, you should not be emotionally involved in the message. If you are emotionally involved, you will not do the right thing. You will fumble and you will make a mistake. You will not deliver the message the way He wants you to deliver it. Once your emotions are in it, you are going to fail. Or, when you are thinking of what the outcome should be. What is your business? Is it your word? Remember, prophetic ministers, you are an instrument. Can this chair tell me where to put it? Can this chair speak? If I stand on it to do something, it cannot talk. It's job is to stay here. This is you and I as a prophet. Your job is to answer to your master. You have no mind. You have no will. You have no emotion. He chooses what He wants to do with you. You are not the one in control, He is. So, if He sends you to deliver a message, the outcome of the message is none of your business. That's why you must submit.

4. The need for recognition must be put to death. Cast down, not destroyed. If you notice, everybody thrives on recognition. We want to be known. This feeling of recognition must bow down to the call. Faithful proclamation of God's word. All of these 4 stages must bring you to the cross. What happens at the cross? The cross is where you must die. Galatians 2:20 says,

***20 I am crucified with Christ: nevertheless I live; yet not I, but Christ liveth in me: and the life which I now live in the flesh I***

***live by the faith of the Son of God, who loved me, and gave himself for me.***

You. Must. Die. I want to ask everyone a question. Is your prophetic calling real? Is the reality of this call coming out as you are reading? You are looking at your life and what you have been through. You are looking at your destiny. Everything that I am reading in this teaching is just digging into my life. If this is the way you feel, then you must stop struggling completely. What do I mean by stop struggling? Trying to put your will and your emotions in the way of what God is trying to do. It's like a swimmer. You have to stop struggling and just let go. The most painful part of this call is that nobody wants to die. We want to hold on to our will, emotions, and our mind. We don't want to die. If you don't want to die, then you can't do it.

Let me give you an example. One Mother's Day, I was coming to the church and one drunkard slammed into my car so hard that it pushed it into the wall. My wife was upset, and she was justified. We didn't do anything wrong. Here is this drunkard talking trash. Every word was a curse word. We didn't do anything wrong, and he is still using these words. My wife was upset. I mean visibly upset. She was shaking. She was saying that we should call 9-1-1 and everything. I just advised her to calm down. I told her before they show up and do all these things, I will be late for church. You are dead. God is your focus. Did it pain me? Oh, yes. I have been trained to ignore my feelings, my stuff, or anything that belongs to me. I've been trained. It's a difficult journey.

I didn't tell anybody about it until I preached the message on Sunday. It was a powerful message and after the service I told everyone what happened to our car. I left the car in the wall and came to church. Did I like the car? Oh, yes. That's why I got another one, but I don't have any feelings attached to it. I'm not saying that you should not like physical things, but don't be attached to anything. Because as a prophet, God can take it from you at any time. If you are attached to anything, you cannot function. You must stop struggling. Don't try to live again.

To die will be difficult because the people around you do not want you to die. The position that you will take will not make sense to them. You don't have, yet you give. You don't even think about yourself again because you are dead. No feelings. No emotions. No will. The old man is no longer in control. Let me give you another clue. My friend that did our house free of charge when the car port burned down, I invited him to my book launch and he didn't come. This guy is loaded with money. He didn't show up.

So when my car caught fire and burned our car port, I was not going to call him. I know that he is in the building business. I just didn't feel like calling him. So, I was coming from church one day about a week after this had happened and the Spirit of God said, "call him". This guy is a person who hardly picks up your call. That's just him because he is very busy. I said to the Holy Spirit, "what if he doesn't answer." God spoke quietly again, "call him". My mind quickly kicked in, "the person that didn't help you."

Because I am dead to mind now, even though my mind is talking, I picked up the phone and I call. To let you know that when you are dead, it is not that your mind and the devil will not talk to you; however, it will not influence your judgment anymore.

So when I called, strangely he picked up the phone. He said how are you, Sir. I said, you know what something happened and I didn't want to disturb you. So I explained the details and he was in shock. He said, "Pastor, where are you?" I said, "I'm on my home from church." He told me that he was somewhere doing some construction and on his way he would stop by my house. He came and looked at the house. He told me he had some traveling to do, but he would send someone to come and look at it. I'm thinking that he would help me to do it and I would pay him back later. So, he called somebody up and the person came. So, I asked the person how much? The person said, "I was instructed not to talk to you." He said, "are you the Pastor?" I said, "yes." He said, "I was instructed not to talk to you". The following Sunday, while I was in church, that brother went to my house and fixed the damages.

So, when we got home that Sunday, I was like, "my goodness. This man, how am I going to pay him. He has done everything." So I called my wife to pray. Since he was traveling again, I said maybe God will tell me what to do before he comes back. You know I walk by faith now, so I have no plan. Wednesday of the same week, he called and spoke to his partner. He told his partner to tell me that what he did for me was a seed. Over $3,000 job. This is a person I will not normally call. This is where prophetic ministry is important. The person God is telling you to talk to, you may not like the person. You may not even want to do anything with that person, but if you obey Him, you will see the results.

You must not try to defend yourself. You are broken. They are many times people have said things about me, but I don't have time to defend myself again. You will not defend yourself. You are just focused on the assignment. You don't have the strength to fight anymore. You are dead. You are not trying to justify anything. Once you are dead, you are dead. A dead man doesn't talk. "This is what I mean." No, you keep quiet. Now, everything about you has failed you. Your fighter is God. So, even if it takes 2 or 3 months for that person to understand they made a mistake, wait. You don't explain yourself to anybody why you do what you do. Let me tell you, the prophetic ministry does not work out of order. Anybody under prophetic anointing that is behaving out of order is not in that ministry. A prophetic anointing is the most disciplined ministry.

You don't move except He tells you to move. Even when you are not guilty. Even when they accuse you wrong. He will tell you to keep quiet. You suffer in silence. You will not complain to anybody. You will not murmur to anybody. You are dead. You must submit yourself humbly and die. Remember Hannah in 1 Samuel. The Bible says, her adversary provoked her sore. Did you hear Hannah talk back to that woman? Was it recorded in the Bible that Hannah replied back to that woman? No, you are dead. Hannah does not have time for that woman. All Hannah has time for is prayer. Seeking God's face, "God help me". "When you help me, my story will change." Arguing with people is a waste of time.

When God blesses this ministry, everyone will fall in line. We are like this because there has not been a significant blessing or God uses someone to raise the dead or open blind eyes. Everyone will be humbled. That's the truth. Who can talk back to Joel Osteen? Success. Who are you when people are lining up every Saturday night to shake his hand? It's when you are not successful that people talk to you anyhow. This is why you must die. When you die, that is when your new season begins. If you are not dead, you will not enter into your new season.

Let's look at Paul. Let's look at 2 Corinthians 12:7. Look at what the Lord said,

***7And lest I should be exalted above measure through the abundance of the revelations, there was given to me a thorn in the flesh, the messenger of Satan to buffet me, lest I should be exalted above measure.***

You must humbly remain dead. God will make sure of that if He loves you. You are not responsive. Remember the Syrophoenician woman in Matthew 15. Jesus Christ said to that woman, "I didn't come for people like you. I came for the children not dogs." The woman said, "well, I'm a dog. I accept my position." "I am dead. Just give me something." You see this is the position that you have to take. Jesus said to everybody, "I have never seen such a great faith." To somebody that says I am a dog. You see the contrast. Physically, she looks like a dog. Spiritually, she has a great faith. So is a prophet, you will look stupid to everyone around you but to God, "hey!, that is my son. That is my daughter in whom I am well pleased."

To everybody you will look like a fool. "Why must you take that?" They don't understand. I am dead. That's why I don't argue with anybody anymore. You are talking from your understanding and your revelation. You will understand better. Revelation brings you confidence. The woman understood that Jesus was the only one that could help her. So when Jesus was calling her a dog, she accepted it. She needed His help and she got it. Nobody wants to be in that position. Everyone wants to prove they are right. God will not use you when you are like that. So, as a prophet, you must humbly die. When you do that, all the noise will cease.

All the turmoil will stop. There will be a great calm that is beyond explanation. Now, I understand why I am always calm when serious problems come. I didn't lose sleep when my two cars got burnt. I didn't have any money, but I knew that God would take care of it. I just had this peace, unspeakable peace like I had a million dollars in my pocket. I was not worried. I was not concerned. God had given me a word before this happened that every storm He would speak peace.

So I stood on that word even when everybody was saying "harass the insurance." I said, "Sir, I don't have any strength to fight." #1 this is our fasting month. I will let God have His way. He gave me the car in the first place. I wasn't qualified for it. He gave it to me. So, if He decides to take it, then He has a better plan. I was just calm. There will be a great calm, and this is the time to let go. All your efforts, you are now dead. When you are now dead, you must allow yourself to be buried. You must wait. There will be a waiting period. Once you are dead, there must be a waiting period. Let's look at Philippians 2:8,

***8And being found in fashion as a man, he humbled himself, and became obedient unto death, even the death of the cross.***

You must be obedient to death. That waiting period, your soul, your will, your mind, and your emotions have to decay. They have to rot. You must die so that they will not rise up again. You know people of God that if Moses would have dealt seriously with that anger, you know it wouldn't have been a problem for him in the future. He didn't deal with that anger. Remember, he used anger to kill somebody earlier on in the beginning of his ministry. That anger did not die in him. Even though he ate with God and talked with God, that anger was still there.

That's why it's so dangerous to not just start but finish. It's possible for everyone to finish if you are ready to die. Let us look at waiting in the book of Lamentations 3:26,

***26It is good that a man should both hope and quietly wait for the salvation of the Lord.***

You must not only wait, but wait quietly. Not mumbling. Not grumbling. Not talking. Quietly. People that are waiting on you do not understand why you are waiting. Let's look at Isaiah 30:18

***[18]And therefore will the Lord wait, that he may be gracious unto you, and therefore will he be exalted, that he may have mercy upon you: for the Lord is a God of judgment: blessed are all they that wait for him.***

If you can wait. People cannot wait for God and that is the problem. God cannot forget you. He does not leave people stranded on the waiting bus stop. You don't wait for God and lose out. He does not forget you. If you can wait. It's difficult, but it's rewarding. Let's read Psalm 69:3

***[3]I am weary of my crying: my throat is dried: mine eyes fail while I wait for my God.***

So, when you are waiting for God, you are going to go through some pain. If I don't tell you the truth, I'm telling you now that waiting on the Lord is not easy. It's not. It's a trying time. I'm begging you by the mercy of God. If you don't wait for Him, your ministry is useless. Remember, He is the One that calls the shots. You are just the instrument. You don't call the shots for your maker. People want to serve God the way they like, the way they feel, "at least I'm trying". They come to church once a week.

They want to justify their weakness and their stagnancy in their spiritual walk. "God understands." That is for babies. That's why some people wait and wait for their blessings and God will see that they are not serious. They are not dependable. You can't count on them. They are not reliable. They can't wait on God. They don't want to cry until their throat is dry and make up their mind to wait. Regardless of what they have to go through because you are convinced beyond shadow of doubt that He is the only One that can help you.

Let's look at Psalm 27:14,

***[14]Wait on the Lord: be of good courage, and he shall strengthen thine heart: wait, I say, on the Lord.***

You must understand that when you wait for God, He will not leave you comfortless. He will encourage you while you are waiting. God is not a wicked God. So wait for your resurrection. After you die, there will be a silent time or a calm in your life. There will be a calm in your life where people will ask you questions and you are just quiet. You are dead now. They will ask you to prophecy and you have nothing to say because you are dead. That's the days when you die. When He wakes you up from that death, there will be new power and new authority. How do I know that? Acts 1: 4

***[4]And, being assembled together with them, commanded them that they should not depart from Jerusalem, but wait for the promise of the Father, which, saith he, ye have heard of me.***

There must be a silent period when all you do is obey. You are just quiet. You are not talking. You are no longer loud in the church. You are just quiet because you are going through a process of waiting. When you resurrect. When the power comes, there is a new ministry and a new beginning. You don't move until that power comes for a new beginning. You don't do anything. You are so quiet. Nobody hears your voice. You are dead. He has finished His work over you. The power will now come and suddenly your ministry will rise up as a full fledge prophet of God and things will begin to happen in a new dimension. Now you are resurrected. A new life. A new boldness. Remember, no man strive without striving lawfully. If you do not strive lawfully then you are striving out of control.

So, you now begin a new walk with the Lord. Now, the strange part of it is that the Bible says from glory to glory. That is one stage of it. When God wants to take you to another level or stage, you have to die again. The process will repeat itself over and over again as you go higher and higher in Him. You keep on dying and He will resurrect you. He will take you to another level or dimension and you die again. He resurrects you. Just like exams. When you finish one degree and you want another degree, there is another exam. As you go higher, the exam becomes harder. Same thing with the prophetic ministry.

# CHAPTER 3

# GOD'S TRAINING FOR THE PROPHETIC OFFICE

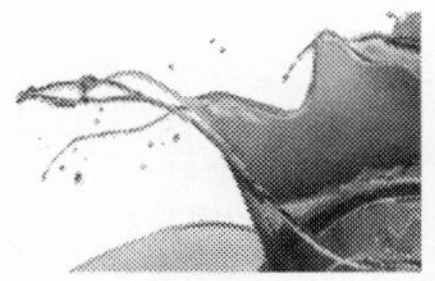

There is no prophet that the LORD called and they said, "Daddy, I'm ready!" No, not a single one. What happens is that God sees in you something that you don't see in yourself and then He makes His choice.

One thing I want to let everybody know is that you are loved by God. He does not choose everybody for this. When God makes you His choice, He will try as hard as possible to make you to do what He wants you to do; but if you are adamant, and you don't want to do it He will eventually leave you alone(Gen. 6:3). When He leaves you alone, you will become more miserable than when you were obeying Him. You will not find fulfillment in any other thing. So, people of God, I want to encourage you in this walk. There is nobody that walks with God and loses. So, what do you have to lose anyway? If God says, "come up with me, hither", it is because He loves you.

See yourself as someone privileged. Amen. I'm trying to encourage you so that you can study more and work harder. See yourself as privileged to be chosen by God to walk this journey with Him. It's a privilege to be used by God in those offices. He doesn't use everybody. He never does, because some people are not willing to go beyond who they are. They want to be in their comfort zone. When you are like that, you are not going to be useful to Him.

The basic teachings that I have shared so far is 50% of what ordinary Christians should go through. This is what we have been called for, to be called out of darkness and into the marvelous light. As a normal child of God, you cannot mix flesh with the Spirit. It's not going to work. Even though we have so many, millions living like that today, there are those who have been chosen to "come up hither", as stated in the book of Revelation chapter 4 verse 1-where it says I heard a voice to come up higher. God wants you to be head and shoulders above everybody else and to see some things that others are not privileged to see. So, in this you become an instrument speaking the mind of God to change lives.

Remember, the reason that Jesus Christ died is to bring us into the fulfillment of our destiny in Christ and not the plan of the enemy any more. So, if we are not living the life that will please God, it makes the death of Jesus Christ null and void.

One of the major reasons that Jesus died was to save us from the sinful nature and to put us on that path of fulfilling His plans for our lives. God sees you and He chose you. You will find out that except the software is corrupt, you all have a good heart. However, your will, emotions, and feelings must die. If you have a good heart and your heart is pure, then you hear some things and you listen to your will, it will corrupt your heart. This is why it is so important as a child of God walking on this level that you must be really, really careful of what you are listening to. It will corrupt your heart. It will corrupt your zeal. It will corrupt your energy and your fire for God. The Bible says, "faith cometh by hearing and hearing the Word of God". So, what you hear determines your faith level. Same thing with what I was saying just now, what you are hearing determines how you serve God.

People will want you to compromise the standard of God in

your life. We will look at how God trains you. So, when we are talking about prophetic ministry, prophetic ministry has to do with the Word of God. Without the Word of God, there is no prophetic ministry. If you no longer speak the Word of God, then you are no longer a true prophet. So, as a prophetic minister, the Word of God is what you live by, breathing it in and breathing it out.

So, what is this Word? We have two levels of this Word. We have the Word – logos and rhema. Logos is the spoken Word. Rhema, is the revealed Word. I can speak logos in the church from now until tomorrow, but if people do not get revelation, it does not become a rhema. Rhema is "I can do all things through Christ that strengthens me" and it changes your outlook towards life totally. That Philippians 4:13 helps you go through your entire life. That is a Rhema. Logos is just a spoken word.

The fact that I speak it does not become a rhema until it is revealed to you. That's why somebody can look at Psalm 23 verse 1 "the Lord is my Shepherd" and preach on it for 30 days using only that statement. That Word has revealed something to him and now God is taking him through some stages of the revealed word, that is Rhema.

That is why we have Christians that are not really fulfilling their destiny because a lot of them hear the Logos every Sunday, but the Word has not become a Rhema in their lives. They have no understanding of revelation knowledge of what that word means. So, they can hear the Logos all they want, but until it becomes a Rhema, you cannot be a doer. Are you getting it? Praise the Lord.

Now we have another level of the Word, gnosis. This is what pertains to your ministry. Gnosis is the revealed word, the revelation knowledge of the Word which is at another level of revelation. Which is, you are given an insight of that word for other people. When there is preaching in the church and you understand the message and you are living by it, it's Rhema because you understand. Gnosis is a Word given to you to give to other people or other individuals. This is the power of knowledge. Gnosis is knowing. Knowing something that other people do not know.

So, the word "knowledge" is knowledge received from the Holy Spirit to enable us to minister effectively to the needs of the people. The prophetic ministry has to do with the word knowledge. To know and to understand circumstances and strategies of the enemy. This prophetic ministry or gnosis helps us to speak the knowledge of God into situations. It helps us to speak the knowledge of God into a situation to surprise, to disarm, to open up, bring answers, healing, and understanding. All these things are what your prophetic anointing does.

- Disarm- reveal information that prevents harm or death to a person.

The Word knowledge according to 1 Corinthians 12: 1-11 is one of the nine gifts in the Bible. Let's go there.

***[1]Now concerning spiritual gifts, brethren, I would not have you ignorant. 2 Ye know that ye were Gentiles, carried away unto these dumb idols, even as ye were led. 3 Wherefore I give you to understand, that no man speaking by the Spirit of God calleth Jesus accursed: and that no man can say that Jesus is the Lord, but by the Holy Ghost.***

No man. There is nobody. If you see anybody that says he is a child of God and does not acknowledge Jesus Christ, that person is a demon. If a person says, "I don't believe in Jesus Christ", then you should know that he does not have the spirit of God. The Holy Spirit will never allow anyone to witness against Jesus. No person. Ok, let me read on.

***[4]Now there are diversities of gifts, but the same Spirit. 5And there are differences of administrations, but the same Lord 6And there are diversities of operations, but it is the same God which worketh all in all.***

So your gifting is to edify the body. It's not a gift to show off or to stand outside of the body. Everything you are doing is to edify the body. Let's continue.

***[7]But the manifestation of the Spirit is given to every man to profit withal***

So, as an intercessor, as a prophet to tell you the truth there is nothing that God gives a man that will not bless you. Not only to profit the church, but personally. There is no true intercessor or a prophet that is called to intercede, or a Pastor, or a teacher that does not profit in it. That's why God tells a man of God to go and meet a woman, I know you are hungry, you are a spiritual man, and you have to feed your body, go and meet somebody that will be a blessing to you. This has been abused in the Kingdom. I have been in that position with someone that I prayed for and God answered the prayer.

They were so excited and suggested a lot of things to me which God did not approve. I had to be careful because before you know it, even though God want us to profit, people will be leading you and not God. So, most of the time the prophet will not sit down in the church, don't want to be taught, or be under any man of God, and you see them all over the street lying to people and taking money from people. It's good to profit with it, but profit with it in a godly way. Don't do any gimmicks or side corners. Amen.

God will ask you in a strange manner or in a strange way to do certain things, and you have to be very careful how you present it. God can ask you to go somewhere for somebody to bless you with money, but you have to make sure that it is God speaking to you. Don't ever do that without double checking. Remember, the flesh does not die at once. It does not die altogether. It does not die once. If you are thinking that your flesh will die once, you are lying to yourself. As a matter of fact, you conquer this area of your life and another area shows up. That's why Paul said, "I die daily." You die until you die finally. Until you die to go to Jesus, you are still dying. To profit withal, it's good to profit with it, but make sure you do it in a godly way. Let's go on.

***[8]For to one is given by the Spirit the word of wisdom; to another the word of knowledge by the same Spirit; [9]To another faith by the same Spirit; to another the gifts of healing by the same Spirit; [10]To another the working of miracles; to another prophecy; to another discerning of spirits; to another divers kinds of tongues; to another the interpretation of tongues:***

One thing that I want to let all of you know about the prophetic ministry, it carries most of this, wisdom, knowledge, faith, gift of healing, the working of miracles, prophecy, and discerning of spirits. The prophetic ministry works in all these and that's why the training is severe. That's why Elisha can tell Naaman go and wash somewhere- healing. That's why Elijah can call fire down- miracles. You understand? It is because they work in all these things. That's why Elijah can say by this time tomorrow, this will happen- word of wisdom.

As a prophetic minister, you operate in most of these gifts. The training is severe and you still give prophecy. Now, some people do not operate in all of these gifts because for each of these gifts, require their own training. That's why the training is very tough especially when you happen to be in a ministry where it is needed, God will train you in every of those areas because you will need it. Amen.

Everything about prophetic is spiritual. You cannot do anything in the physical with it. Once you are physical, it automatically kills the incense and the purpose of the anointing. The anointing does not work effectively outside of the Holy Spirit. The Holy Spirit is like your oil or your engine. Once you are not in tune with Him, you are out of tune. Once you are out of tune, it's like listening to your Christian station 89.3 on 89.4. You will not hear it. All you hear is "crack, crack, crack, crack". This is where accuracy is very important. You cannot mix something up. It's not going to work. Once you are outside of that boundary of the spiritual, you are in the flesh.

Another reason your position is so important is because you are a carrier of God's word. God uses you to bring Christ into every situation. Any situation that is full of turmoil and mess, when God gives you revelation, you speak the Word of God (which is Jesus according to John 1:1), you bring Christ into the situation and wherever Christ is, there is a solution. This is why you are so important because you are a representative of God here on Earth.

Do you see why it is so important about how you act in the church? People are looking at you. Have you found out that you are so attracted to people? The way you do in the church, the way you behave in the church is what will make other people behave. You have this unusual attraction to yourself. Sometimes instead of worshipping God, they are watching you. When they see that you are worshipping, then they begin to worship. That's the truth.

Why? Because of the aura of God around and inside of you, you attract attention. People look at you as a stepping stone to wherever they want to go.

This is why you cannot become corrupted because you have been bought by an incorruptible seed. If you are corrupted, you can corrupt the whole church with your false information. You see my point? That's why it's so important that you read very well, so you don't tell people what is wrong or speak on behalf of the Pastor or the leader when you don't know. You can corrupt people with wrong information because they will listen to you. You carry an aura and the people will want to go to you. Remember, this thing is spiritual. You won't know you carry it, but they know. So, even when you don't ask them, they still come to you and ask you about things. This is why you must have correct information. Don't just say things that you are not sure of because they will run with it and it will corrupt even more people. A little unleaven, leavens all.

Now, this is where this gets serious. You are not only called to affect your immediate environment, you are called to affect humanity. So, your life becomes a sign for humanity. You wonder why people are interested in your life more than anybody else. The aura. You cannot explain it. Sometimes you try to hide and they still come and meet you where you are hiding. You have been chosen by God. Remember, it doesn't matter the size. Remember, it doesn't matter the age. Remember, it doesn't matter what you are wearing. Once God has chosen you, age and all those things does not matter. They will still come and meet you. Have you thought about it? How will old people vast in the knowledge of God sit down with a 12 year old for 3 days? Have you thought about it? These are not young Christians. These are leaders. They didn't sit down with their Pastor like that. After the service has ended, they now sat down with Jesus for 3 days. Jesus carries an aura. That's why you must be a good example. You see, they accuse Jesus in every area but they could not accuse Him of being disrespectful to His father or His mother. After that day, He went to be subject to His parents. This is why the training is very important because they training makes you (even with the anointing and the grace you carry) to be very submissive.

Remember, you don't have your own life anymore. You are dead. You are an instrument. He can decide to use you. He can decide not to use you. God reserves the right not to use you for the next 3 years. If He doesn't say anything to you, that does not make you no more prophet. He reserves the right. This is where a lot of people miss it. That's why they can't stay in a church. Once they cannot say anything to anybody nor do anything for anybody, they think the anointing is useless. No, it's not. He reserves the right to use you or not. When He decides to use you, He will give you information that will affect a whole humanity.

Did we ever know who Jonah was before God called him? We don't even know where he came from. This is where the journey now gets serious because He is the God Almighty. He reserves the right not to speak to you about anything for the next 5 years and when He decides to speak to you again, it's just to tell you to do one crazy thing again. That is it. He's God. Remember, you are just an instrument. It's just like some of us have things in our house that you bought with your money, for example, like a picture. Since we locked them in a room, they cannot come out until they are moved again. Does that mean that those pictures are no longer appreciated? They are still appreciated, but they must stay there until we are ready to use them again. That's what an instrument is. So, we must understand.

The Word knowledge is a thought, impression on a vision, or

a direct audible voice of the Holy Spirit about a situation, circumstance which is not learned through a human effort or mind. Word of knowledge is a thought and you don't even know where the thought came from. How you came up with that information is not because you had prior knowledge of anything. Sometimes, you have not ever met the man or the woman in that situation before in your life. You will just have this thought in your heart. You don't know how it came about. So, this how the Word of Knowledge is. It is also a fragment of information given by God. Remember, you don't prophecy all. You prophecy in part. That's why with all the gift of prophecy I have; there are some things in this church that I will still not know, and that doesn't make me less prophetic. You cannot know everything. There are some things that I do not know until God reveals it to me. Praise the Lord. Hallelujah. In Jesus Name. Amen.

# CHAPTER 4

# HOW TO FUNCTION AS A PROPHETIC MINISTER

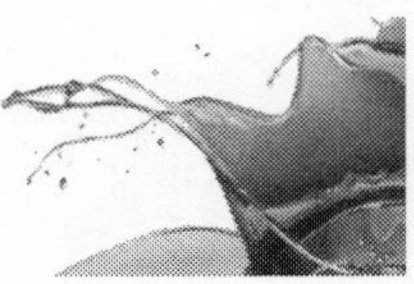

We are going to continue our look at the Word of knowledge. The Word of knowledge is information given by God disclosing the truths which the Holy Spirit wishes to make known concerning a particular person or a situation.

Now, to flow in the Word of Knowledge in the prophetic ministry, we must be willing and available to obey the Holy Spirit. If you are not obeying the Holy Spirit, you cannot properly flow in that gift. You must be able to identify the Holy Spirit and I want to encourage you that the way to identify the voice of God is by reading the Word of God silently to yourself. Not novels or textbooks, but the Word of God. Don't forget that we see out of our mind. With our mind, we can read anything, but it is only the Spirit of God that will help our mind to read the Word of God clearly with understanding. Your mind can still read, but the mind will not find any pleasure in reading the Bible. If you are reading the Word of God with just your mind, after reading 5 sentences, your mind will say to just throw out this, it's no good. It's not working and you don't understand what you are reading. That's your mind. Then you pick up a newspaper, and your mind finds pleasure or is excited to read that one.

Your mind is still the part of yourself that is carnal. This is why the bible says that we should have the mind of Christ. The mind of Christ wants to read the Word of God. The carnal man does not want to read the Word of God. The mind of Christ will say give your best to God. The carnal man will say take care of your bills first before you take care of God. You see the difference? This is how you know the difference between the carnal and the spiritual man. The carnal man is very selfish. "You do for yourself first." "Nobody knows what's going on." You forget that there is a God that is watching and seeing everything that you are doing. The carnal man will not let you understand that God is seeing everything that you are doing and every move that you are making. The carnal man will be teaching you how to sidetrack obedience and how to short change God. That's what he will be planning with you. The carnal man will tell you, "Don't pay tithes this week. Pay your bills first." "God understands." So, the carnal man will give you ways to short change God. The spiritual man would never advise you like that, never.

We must be able to identify when you are carnal and when you are spiritual. If you don't know the difference, you will miss God all the time. Let me give you the secret of the carnal man, he is very, very self-centered. He will never let you make any effort to obey God. He will tell you, "you don't have to do that." "Are you the Pastor? Are you the leader? You are doing the best you can. At least you are coming to church. Why must you invite anybody? Let Pastor do that. He's praying." He will be giving you logical reasons to disobey God and not to make any efforts. The mind will say, "why must I read my Bible. Pastor is not calling me to preach. I don't need to study. I'm not teaching bible study." That's the carnal mind.

The carnal mind will tell you things to stagnate you spiritually. Remember, the carnal mind is an enemy to God. So, he will never let you make any efforts towards your spiritual life. If you enjoy your comfort zone of not doing anything, you will enjoy it because it is good to the flesh. Remember, sugar is good to the flesh. Hello?

I had to cut myself off from soda. One day, some time ago, I drank about 2 or 3 sodas in one function. It was so sweet to my mouth and I was amazed at how it was just going down. Until this day, I hardly drink soda. No more. I prefer juice or PowerAde. The soda is so sweet and it's killing you. Diabetes is coming. It's so sweet and so damaging to the body. Sixteen teaspoons of sugar are in one can of soda. This is what the carnal mind does to the spiritual man. It will decay and you will enjoy it because it's making you not to obey God. It's good to the flesh because it is what you really want to do. The Lord will help us. In Jesus Name.

This means you receive the Word by faith, through the prompting of the Holy Spirit. It will make the information known. Remember, it's two stages. The information is given first. Most people move the moment the information is given and that is wrong. The information is first of all given, then make sure you are prompted by the Holy Spirit to deliver it and when to deliver it.

I've seen some people act out of order, even with men of God. In a meeting, I've seen them raise up their hand saying "God is telling me something". Why would you do that? The fact that the information is given it's not meant to be shared immediately. Now, after the information has been given this is where self-control comes in. Remember, the calling is not to show off. The calling is to be an instrument for God. So, sometimes the flesh wants to show off. The moment you get the information, the flesh will want you to tell what God is saying, and you just kill yourself.

As a prophetic minister if you are based on flesh and you want to show off, you just self-destruct. You put a time bomb on yourself and you self-destruct. Eventually, nobody wants to do anything with you because you don't have character with the anointing. Anointing without character is a useless anointing. Most of the time when you have anointing and you don't have self-control, it becomes a problem, a big one.

How do you function correctly in this prophetic office?

1. Have a strong desire to please the Holy Spirit. The only way you can function correctly, (now we are going from stage to stage. Now you are dead), is to please the Holy Spirit. You know I told you

that you can't kill the flesh at once, only Jesus Christ can do that. He said in the book of John, "it is finished". When He said that it is finished, everything has come to an end. Everything that has to do with my salvation and your salvation was completed. For me and you, because we are still in this uniform, we have to die daily. You must have a very strong desire to please the Holy Spirit. You must fall in love with the Holy Spirit. You will never do anything that the Holy Spirit has not told you to do. It doesn't matter how it feels to your flesh. The Holy Spirit becomes major for you. If the Holy Spirit does not say it, you are not going to move. Even though the message is at the tip of your tongue and the Holy Spirit says "don't share it", you don't. This is where discipline comes in. You must be very, very disciplined with the anointing.

2. You must be very, very disciplined. Your self-control must be at 200% even when every other child of God is at 100%, yours must be 200% because there are going to be certain situations, certain times that God will give you revelation and you know what the Lord is saying and He is saying to you, "keep quiet" and that person is standing right beside you. Have you ever heard people say, "I didn't want to share anything but I was discussing with that person and that person said something about it, so I decided to share it." You are on your own.

This has happened to me. I have been guilty of that before. I have shared things with people. I had a revelation and the person was talking to me and our discussion went to that point and I share the revelation. After I shared it, I got into my car and the Spirit of God said, "who told you to tell him?" "Did I tell you to tell him?" The Holy Spirit is so powerful. All of our explanations that we give, He doesn't want to hear that. You know we are very defensive naturally. How do I know that? Go back to Adam and Eve. God, "Why did you eat the fruit?". Adam, "It's not me 'oh, it was Eve." God, "Eve, why did you eat?". Eve, "No, no, it was the devil." So, naturally after that fall, after their eyes became open, we are naturally defensive. This is why you see people in years and years of self-denial that they have a bad attitude. They will defend themselves to the end even when it is obvious. They will still say, "I am not like that." All the Holy Spirit wants you to do is acknowledge that you are wrong.

One thing about the Holy Spirit is that once you do not acknowledge that mistake, He may not speak to you for the next two weeks until you reconcile back to that position that you used to be with Him. The moment you repent and get yourself back to that position, He deals with you as if nothing has happened before. He will talk to you as if nothing happened yesterday. That's one thing about the Holy Spirit. That's why I love him so much. Once your repentance is sincere, He will just continue from where both of you stopped and continue the conversation. He will not even make reference to it anymore. That's why you should have Him as your Comforter, as your Friend.

He gave me peace throughout that event. I didn't know how God would work it all out. I didn't know how I was going to be restored with the car, but He just gave me peace. He told me "I will speak to every storm. Remember? So, don't worry." I just left it like that. So, we must understand when He speaks have self-discipline. Your self-discipline must be very, very strong.

3. Be sensitive to God. Know what you can do to grieve Him. Know what you can say that will grieve Him. Know how you can behave that will grieve Him. You must be sensitive to His leading. When somebody is talking about things that will spoil your spirit or that will make you to be disconnected from the Holy Spirit, don't continue that conversation. Some people will just come and when they see you like this, everything they are saying is negative, it grieves the spirit. So, I just cut the conversation off. You want to keep your spirit at the level in where you can hear Him. Remember, even God will not look at Jesus with sin on Him. So, you can imagine what He does with the Holy Spirit when we fall into sin again and again. It just cuts off the communication process. The Holy Spirit, the Bible says, is the only One that when you sin against Him, there is no forgiveness. So, you don't want to

blaspheme against Him.

You grieve Him, make sure you reconcile immediately. Some people are out of touch with the Holy Spirit for a long time and they don't even know it because they are so used to their flesh. They listen to their flesh 24/7. Be sensitive to God.

4. Know or recognize when the Holy Spirit is speaking about a person or a matter. Remember, your will, your emotions, everything about you has been dead. Know when the Holy Spirit is speaking rather than your thoughts or your flesh about a matter or a person. You must recognize because there are other voices that speak. If the devil can speak to Jesus, he will speak to you. So, if we say that we don't hear from the devil, we are deceiving ourselves. The devil has no respect for anybody. Amen. If he can go to Heaven, why can't he go to your house? They were calling a meeting of the children of God and he showed up there without an invitation, and he took over the conversation in the book of Job.

That's why I don't like people that are too forward. The Spirit of God is gentle. The devil took over the conversations, "I've been going to and fro." Even the children that were there didn't say anything. Go and read that story. It says when the children of God gathered, they didn't invite them. So, you want to be careful with people that come to church with a strange fire and just want to be known. That's not the spirit of God. Remember, the Bible clearly says, your gift will make room for you. If you are really, really gifted, people will not be able to do without you. You don't have to show off, you are needed for this work.

That's why it is necessary for you to pray about the ministry that you are in. It should not be the Pastor alone with information. You, too, should be bringing information to the Pastor about how to expand and grow the ministry. Pray, and when you open yourself up to God, He will tell you. He says His secrets are revealed to His prophets. He will tell you what He has told the Pastor for confirmation. Sometimes when the encouragement comes from the Pastor alone, it becomes hard to receive. The members are used to the Pastor encouraging them, but when it comes from the leaders or ministers, they will believe it. So, pray and ask the Lord to speak to you.

5. Know the right time to make the information known. Now, you should not come and meet the Pastor as soon as the service has ended on the way to his office and you begin to tell what the Lord showed you in front of everyone. That is a show off. Know the timing. Know when to share information. No matter how excited you feel about the information, enter the office with the Pastor and then say what you want to say. By speaking in front of everybody, you have just let your Pastor know that you are not ready for the prophetic ministry. That's a show off. One of the bad things about prophetic ministry is when your flesh begin to show off like that, you will not be used by God anymore. Now, you will be hearing other voices, but it's not from God anymore. Remember false prophets, they hear too, but they are hearing from somebody else. The Bible says, "who has said when the Lord has not said?" Does it not say that in the book of Ezekiel? So, you must understand that this is serious.

One of the true attributes of a true prophet is that you must be humble. Remember, you are broken. You are dead, and anybody dead will not do that. It is when your Pastor tells you to share is when you share. Remember, God gave you that gift. If He wants you to be prominent, then He will be the One to make you prominent. So even after the Lord has revealed something to you, before Sunday service the same spirit that worketh in you to will and to do, will come and meet your Pastor and remind him/her of the agreement. He's the same Spirit now, right? Now if the Spirit of Lord gave you information to share and you don't want to share it, you are walking in disobedience, and He reserves the right to punish you however He sees right. The Holy Spirit will give you the right timing. Let me give you a powerful example in the Bible so you will understand what I'm talking about.

Remember Esther. When she had access to the King, if she was not a girl that had been well brought up, the moment she would have gotten before the King, she would have been shouting about Haaman wanting to kill her people. No, she didn't do that. Even when the King offered her up to half his kingdom, she still refused to speak. That is self-control. That's why I respect Esther, very, very much. It takes a woman of self-control not to talk. Knowing the danger that was lurking around the corner in a few days and she has that kind of access, she could have just spilled the beans all on the floor in front of the wrong people. Remember, coming before the King alone is an abomination. The rulers of the nation are looking at the king asking why he won't kill this one. This the 2nd time, they are disrespecting you. Why did you not kill this one?

Esther was wise. She needed the king's attention alone. "King, can you come and eat at my house?" King, "yes, sure. Is that why you came in?" Esther, "yes, sir." King, "It's granted." The King went, ate the first night. The King asks, "what do you want me to do?". Esther said, "King can you come again, Sir and I want you to bring Haaman this time around." Wise woman. She first of all made the King comfortable.

Women are very, very influential. Whether we like it or not, women influence men's decisions. Women, very powerful. There's no action of a man that is not influenced by a woman. As disciplined as I am, my wife still influences my behavior. Not to people, but to some things in the house. Not spiritually, but naturally in dealing with things at home. What she feels matters to me. So as an influential woman, don't use your power anyhow. Women are very influential to the ministry. That's why you see more women in the ministry than men.

Know the right time to give information. Have self-control. As a leader or head of department, go to the office of your Pastor. Show some respect and discuss the situation. Don't talk about your department in front of people at any time. Give that position some respect.

6. Know how to minister the Word in an edifying way. There is some information that the Lord will give you like Prophet Moses, if you go and read that in Exodus 25, the Lord commanded Moses, "tell the people to give". When Moses went to pass that information on, he said, "whoever is willing". Wisdom. So you must be very, very careful. There are some things that the Lord has told me to tell people. I didn't say it exactly the way God said it, I had to use wisdom as a man of God. Not to change the message, but to say it in a way that will not hurt the person.

Let me give you an example. Look at the message the prophet went to give Hezekiah. He didn't say God is going to kill you. He said "prepare your house for this sickness is unto death." He didn't say, "God told me to tell you that He will kill you." That's two different things. Do you understand? You must apply wisdom not to change the message, but the Holy Spirit is the owner of language, right, the Holy Spirit will give you the words to use without damaging the assignment or the instruction. Amen.

7. Be willing and prepared to accept any teaching, any fine tuning, or correction from those over you in the Lord. No matter how good you are as a prophet, you must be prepare to receive fine tuning, correction, teaching, or any other thing that they want to give unto you. Let us look at the Word of God concerning that.

Let's go to Romans 1 and see what Brother Paul said, a very, very powerful statement. Romans 1:11,

***For I long to see you, that I may impart unto you some spiritual gift, to the end ye may be established;***

So, there will always be a reason to correct, fine tune, and teach so that you can be established in that gift. So when you see a fake prophet, you can identify one because you have been taught. So when you see people operating in their gift, you won't get carried away. You can sit down and watch them very well. The Bible says, test every spirit. That's why I don't get moved when people jump around and prophecy. That doesn't mean, it's coming from God. Do you understand what I'm saying? You must be impacted and apt to teach. You must be ready to receive teaching all the time because all of us are growing. Praise the Lord.

8. Take responsibility for the effect of the Word of Knowledge after the delivery. You owe nobody an apology when you have heard what the Holy Spirit said for you to deliver. What I mean is that, if you deliver the message and the person that you told insulted you, don't feel bad. Don't feel bad except you are not sure it came from God. If it comes from God, accept the insult because remember, you are representing somebody. So, if they insult you, they are not insulting you, they are insulting God. What did Jesus Christ say, when they slap you, turn the left one, right.

You cannot speak against a prophet of God and go scott free. The Bible says, Moses was the meekest on the face of the Earth. When Aaron and Miriam accused him wrongly, did Moses say a word? No, but God still judged them. They suffered for it harshly. So be careful. Anyone that carries prophetic anointing, or apostolic anointing, don't open your mouth against them. That's why it's good to pray. Go to God. Go to your closet and pray. Don't even talk to anybody about it. It's dangerous except that person is not carrying the grace of God upon his life.

One thing I want to let all of us know is that a lot of time people uses physical to judge a man with his grace and it's very, very wrong. The fact that you carry the grace of God does not mean that everything around you will be rosy. The fact that God has chosen you does not mean that everything will be smooth. People, most of the time, when they see that nothing is smooth around you, they say, "he says he is called of God." "Why, why, why?" It's a lie. It's only a carnal man that will use eyes of physical to judge spiritual things. Do you understand what I'm saying?

One thing I want everyone to realize is that the training of every man of God or every child of God is different. The Lord did not tell Isaac to kill any of his children. He didn't tell Jacob to do that. He didn't tell Abraham to sow on a dry ground. Isaac did not have to fight with any angels. Yet, throughout the Old Testament, God was boasting about the 3 of them. I am the Father of Abraham, Isaac, and Jacob. You would think that they did such great things. For me, if I were God, I would only boast about Abraham because those two did not go through anything. To sow on a dry ground. Is that as bad as waiting for God for 25 years? Within a year, the Bible says, Isaac reaped and he grew bigger and bigger. So, in the space of 2 to 3 years, he has been blessed.

Abraham had to face servant having children abundantly, blessing their children every Sunday, every Wednesday, and he doesn't have any child to show for it for 25 years. That's the most mental torture he could ever experience. Even Jacob, he was having children abundantly. The only thing he had to do was fight one night and he got his blessing. Even when he was under Laban, he was still being blessed. He was not suffering, but Abraham the mental torture of being called the "father of nations", and yet with none. It was terrible and not only that, but he had to endure it until he was a 100 years old.

He was not called into ministry until the age of 75. So, I respect Abraham more than all those young ones because they didn't have to go through what Abraham went through. God still boast about the 3 of them throughout the Bible all the time. They didn't go through the same exam, but unfortunately you see Christians judging the book before they open it.

Let's read Jeremiah 1:7-8 to close with that.

***[7]But the Lord said unto me, Say not, I am a child: for thou shalt go to all that I shall send thee, and whatsoever I command thee thou shalt speak. [8]Be not afraid of their faces: for I am with thee to deliver thee, saith the Lord.***

So, you should not be afraid of the consequences that will come after the delivery of the message. Bear it, knowing that God is with you. If you are sure that He is the One that sent you on that errand, be sure that He will never leave you. He will never disappoint you. He will never forsake you. He said, "Jeremiah, don't worry, I am with you." So, if you have that confidence that He is with you, then you deliver that message with utmost respect, and don't worry yourself about the repercussion because it's not your word anyway, except it is your word. If it is your word, then you can be worried, but since it is not your word, you are not guilty. The One that has sent is the most guilty. So, don't worry yourself. Clean your face and go. Amen. That's why the prophet was not ashamed to go into Hezekiah's house again and say, "the Lord has told me to tell you this again". "He's going to heal you. He's going to give you 15 years." He's not ashamed because it was not his word in the first place that Hezekiah was going to die and it is not his word that Hezekiah will live long. He's just a messenger. Remember, your personal title is a delivery person. You just deliver the package. Whatever it is, it's none of your business, just deliver the package. May the Lord bless you, In Jesus Name.

# CHAPTER 5

# HEARING AS A PROPHET

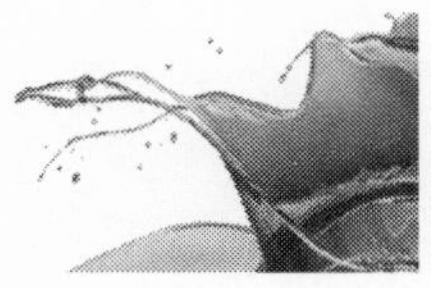

As a prophet, we must hear the voice of the Lord. Let's look at Jeremiah 7:23-24

***23But this thing commanded I them, saying, Obey my voice, and I will be your God, and ye shall be my people: and walk ye in all the ways that I have commanded you, that it may be well unto you. 24But they hearkened not, nor inclined their ear, but walked in the counsels and in the imagination of their evil heart, and went backward, and not forward***

Each time we are not hearing God or doing the will of God, that person is going backward instead of going forward. That is what you call a backslider. A backslider is a person who does not obey the voice of God anymore. We see that God is very particular in how we serve Him. He said, "this thing I commanded, obey my voice". There's no short cut to it. "I will be your God, and ye shall be my people". So the only way to be God's people is when you obey His voice.

In Jeremiah 29:12-13

***12"Then shall ye call upon me, and ye shall go and pray unto me, and I will hearken unto you. 13And ye shall seek me, and find me, when ye shall search for me with all of your heart.*** Amen

One thing I want to let you know is that you are God's people and when you seek for God with all your heart, that's when you will find Him. That means seeking God requires effort. You cannot seek God the way you feel you should seek God. You must seek God with all of your heart.

In Isaiah 30:21 says something very important.

***[21]And thine ears shall hear a word behind thee, saying, This is the way, walk ye in it, when ye turn to the right hand, and when ye turn to the left.***

Every born again Christian, hears the voice of God. You cannot become a born again Christian without hearing God's voice.

There is an example in the book of John 6:44- 46.

***[44]No man can come to me, except the Father which hath sent me draw him: and I will raise him up at the last day. [45]It is written in the prophets, And they shall be all taught of God. Every man therefore that hath heard, and hath learned of the Father, cometh unto me. [46]Not that any man hath seen the Father, save he which is of God, he hath seen the Father.***

So, no man can come to Jesus Christ without being drawn by the Father. So, everyone that has given their lives to Christ, must have heard a voice. Now, the grace to continue on that road is your choice. Once you hear that voice and give your life to Christ, the grace that you receive in the beginning is not able to sustain you for the rest of the journey. That's why we need to go through the process of sanctification.

That's why when Jesus Christ walked with the disciples, even after they have been breathed upon, they still needed to wait on that promise in Jerusalem. If they did not receive that promise and that anointing and that power in Jerusalem, they could not continue that journey. Jesus told them to go and wait in order to be endured by power through the Holy Ghost.

So that means the grace that they had knowing Jesus Christ is not able to carry them through the ministry. So, they needed another grace. Another empowerment. That's why it's important that every child of God, when you are born again, you also have to be filled with the Holy Ghost because that is what will help you on that journey.

So the call of salvation and hearing the voice of God is basic to every child of God, but the general hearing of the voice of God is different from the prophetic ministry. Prophetic ministry is deeper. The Bible clearly tells us that He will send the Comforter that will guide us into all truth, that will give us basic information. The fact that the Holy Spirit is giving you basic information that does not mean that you are a prophet. Amen.

Holy Spirit just gives you information that guides you, that teaches you of how to seek God, how to pray, don't do this, don't do that, but that does not make you a prophet. Prophetic anointing is different. You are hearing God for a specific situation, specific circumstances for a people, a group of people, or an individual.

So, the Spirit of God is the only way that we have some understanding and revelation of who we are in Christ and that's why we have 1 Corinthians 2:9-12. This particular scripture tells us that the Spirit of God gives us revelation of the deep things of God. It is only the Spirit of God that gives us deep revelation of who God is, how to walk with God, and the importance of why we should walk with God.

**[9]But as it is *written, Eye hath not seen, nor ears have heard, neither have entered into the heart of man, the things which God hath prepared for them that love him. [10]But God hath revealed them unto us by his Spirit: for the Spirit searcheth all things, yea, the deep things of God.***

So, the deep things of God can only be revealed by the Spirit of God. There are some things that you will never know, no matter how you fast or how you pray, until the Spirit of God reveals it to you, you will not have that information. Amen. You cannot know it by head knowledge. You cannot know it by reading. You can only know it by the Spirit of God. Amen.

There are 7 major ways that God has revealed of how a prophet can hear. The first one is by the spiritual urim and thummin. The urim basically is like stones embedded in the priest ephod. They put their hand into it and anytime God wants them to reveal information or say that someone's guilty or innocent, they put their hand into that and whichever stone that they touch, that's the one that proves the innocence or the guilt of that person. Any time they touch urim, urim confirms the guilt of that person. When they touch the thummin, it proves the innocence of that person. How do we know that? The urim and thummin were used by the prophets of the Old Testament.

Now the prophets of these days do not carry urim and thummin anymore. That's why the Lord ministered to me that we use a spiritual urim and thummin. Let's read Exodus 28:30

***[30]And thou shalt put in the breastplate of judgment the Urim and the Thummim; and they shall be upon Aaron's heart, when he goeth in before the LORD: and Aaron shall bear the judgment of the children of Israel upon his heart before the LORD continually.***

So the urim and the thummin are the stones that are embedded in the breastplate of the ephad of the priest or the prophets of that time that the Lord used for them to minister. Let's read Leviticus 8 v 8

***8.And he put the breastplate upon him: also he put in the breastplate the Urim and the Thummim.***

Let's also look at Numbers 27:21. People of God, you are getting some good food here because a lot of prayer and research went into this to do this very well so that you will have solid information and you can go before anyone and argue and speak boldly about what is being taught.

***21And he shall stand before Eleazar the priest, who shall ask counsel for him after the judgment of Urim before the LORD: at his word shall they go out, and at his word they shall come in, both he, and all the children of Israel with him, even all the congregation.***

This is the why the position of prophet is so important. Look at what the Bible says. It says, by His word. They shall go out and by His word, they shall come in.

So, your position as a prophet it is very vital and that is why the training, the commitment, and what you have to go through is very serious because you are representing God in His entirety. Whatever comes out of your mouth, people believe it comes from God. That's why you have to live a righteous life, a holy life, and not get involved in fleshy stuff. Because you carry that Word, that Word can work against you if you are not living a righteous life.

Let's look at 1 Samuel 28:6

***6And when Saul enquired of the LORD, the LORD answered***

***him not, neither by dreams, nor by Urim, nor by prophets.***

So, the way God talked to people at that time is by these 2 stones and if they don't get an answer from these 2 stones that means that God is not speaking. Urim proves guilt and thummin proves innocence.

Another example in 1 Samuel 23:9

***[9]And David knew that Saul secretly practised mischief against him; and he said to Abiathar the priest, Bring hither the ephod.***

That means God confirmed it by urim. That's why David asked for the ephod because inside the ephod is where the urim and thummin reside. Praise the Lord. Amen.

Now, how do we translate into spiritual thummin and urim? As a very basic child of God, you will find out that there is something inside of you that either gives you a go ahead to do something or a withdrawal. You cannot explain it. Some of us say, "something tells me" or "I just feel". No, we just don't feel. Since the veil was broken when Jesus Christ died, we now have access to urim and thummin by ourselves.

So because we have that access, we will discover that sometimes as a child of God you want to take a step and you see yourself drawing back. You don't know what is drawing you back, you just feel uncomfortable in your spiritual urim saying, "don't do it".

The same thing with the thummin. Sometimes you want to do something and you see that all your body goes into it. That is your thummin working declaring that the step you are taking is good, innocent, nothing carnal about it. That is how you confirm and walk in this level of relationship, but this urim and thummin is just the basic for every child of God.

The only difference between this urim and thummin in a prophet is that it is the sensitivity and the feeling that is stronger. You can feel that for somebody else more than yourself. So the urim and thummin in a prophet is stronger than in a basic child of God. You feel that for somebody even when they want to do something, you will now say, the Lord said, "you should not do that". Your spiritual urim has said "no" and you just speak it out.

Remember in the beginning of this training process, we said that our will, feelings, and emotions must die. If you are not dead, then your spiritual urim and thummin will not work for anybody else. It will work basically for you, but you will not be able to hear them when it concerns other people. Because you have not developed yourself in that area which means that you are still struggling with your emotions, still struggling with your feelings, so when it comes to somebody else, you cannot judge correctly. Your emotions are still involved.

Your spiritual urim and thummin is not really active to bless other people and when you do, when you have developed yourself or you have totally surrendered yourself in the area of your flesh to be able to walk in that level. So let's look at Luke 23:45

***45And the sun was darkened, and the veil of the temple was rent in the midst.***

The moment the veil was rent, as children of God, we have access to that urim and thummin. Before, it was only the priests that could go behind the veil to tell you what is going on. As a matter of fact, in that olden time, if you read in the book of Deuteronomy and Leviticus, they will tie a chain at the feet of the priests as he is walking inside of that veil. Sometimes, they will put a bell around their robe and they will hear the bell and the chain moving. The moment they stop hearing the bell, they know the priest is dead and they will just use the chain to pull him out. Nobody else can go in there.

This is why it is very awesome when this phenomenon happened when Jesus Christ passed away. He gave everyone access. Now, because He has given everyone access, everyone has the basic urim and thummin, but you as a prophet have killed your flesh more than a basic child of God, you can now use your spiritual urim and thummin to bless other people. Just by the way you feel, in your "gut feeling" what they are about to do is not good.

You will not even say I feel, you will just say that the Lord said you should not do that because you have developed your urim and thummin to that level and you are able to declare the word of the Lord directly. Praise the Lord.

Now, that this gives us a deeper understanding we can look at 1 Corinthians 2:9-12 now has a link to the urim and thummin because we read in that verse that the Spirit of God searcheth the deep things of God, knoweth the mind of God, and knows what God wants us to do. Now the spiritual urim and thummin is developed to a point that you are able to tell some things. Praise the Lord. This is the first level of hearing.

Now if you have not trained yourself to be a blessing to others, don't try and do it because you will just mix your feelings plus your emotions to deliver the message and you will not get the right answer. Amen.

2. Let's go to dreams and visions. God also uses dreams and

visions to speak to His prophets. How do we know that? We know that through the book of Numbers 12:1-8

***1 And Miriam and Aaron spake against Moses because of the***
***Ethiopian woman whom he had married: for he had married***
***an Ethiopian woman. 2 And they said, Hath the LORD indeed***
***spoken only by Moses? hath he not spoken also by us? And***
***the LORD heard it. 3 (Now the man Moses was very meek,***
***above all the men which were upon the face of the earth.)***
***4 And the LORD spake suddenly unto Moses, and unto Aaron,***
***and unto Miriam, Come out ye three unto the tabernacle of***
***the congregation. And they three came out. 5 And***
***the LORD came down in the pillar of the cloud, and stood in***
***the door of the tabernacle, and called Aaron and Miriam: and***
***they both came forth. 6 And he said, Hear now my words: If***
***there be a prophet among you, I the LORD will make myself***
***known unto him in a vision, and will speak unto him in a***
***dream. 7 My servant Moses is not so, who is faithful in all***
***mine house. 8 With him will I speak mouth to mouth, even***
***apparently, and not in dark speeches; and the similitude of***
***the LORD shall he behold: wherefore then were ye not afraid***
***to speak against my servant Moses?***

This is why it is very dangerous to speak against a man of God that carries anointing. This means Moses did not speak for himself.

So God uses visions and dreams to speak to His prophets. One thing that is different about Moses is that God was just trying to let them know that Moses is beyond that level. That He speaks to Moses mouth to mouth and not even in their category. Praise the Lord, but that's not where we are going.

I just wanted to show you that God, Himself said, "I speak to them in dreams and visions." This makes us to know that in the Bible, God speaks to prophets and He will still do the same thing now to any one of you in dreams and in visions. I pray that the Lord will open your eyes to see. As you close your eyes, it's not that you are imagining it, but as you close your eyes, you will see in the spirit. Sometimes I see with my eyes open. You will see their shadows. As you train, your eyes will see those things. Amen.

Your spirit communicates through your senses to your mind. Now, this place is so important because dreams and visions are used to communicate to your mind. Touch, taste, sight, hearing and smell. So, in this dream and vision, the Spirit borrows your sight to communicate to your mind. The Spirit using the 5 senses to communicate to us even in the spiritual level is very powerful and deeper. Just as we have 5 senses, the Spirit has 5 senses that take over the mind with the mind of Christ. We have a mind, but God said to lose our own mind and take His mind.

So everything the enemy has, God has the original. The enemy just has the counterfeit. Praise the Lord. Amen. He will use what you see when you sleep or with your eyes to communicate a message to you as a child of God or a prophet. Visions are an influence that comes from the Spirit that God uses to communicate to you. You have dreams when you are asleep and visions while you are awake. In visions, it may look as if you are sleeping, but you are awake. You will be able to tell some things. For example, one time I was praying with somebody and I saw something upon that person, and the Lord said that what I was seeing on top of the person's head was favor. He said that she was carrying favor.

So, you can see images and God will interpret the meaning for you. This is why visions are so interesting because sometimes it will be as if you are in a trance and you just see some things. You know that you are not sleeping but awake, but it is a vision. God will use dreams and visions to communicate with us to give us revelation for our assignment. In Jesus Name.

3. Prophetic utterance, you know He uses our senses, is something that comes deep within you. You did not plan to say it. It just comes out. I'm not talking about someone that is in the flesh, now. I'm talking about somebody who is powerfully and spiritually inclined. It comes from your belly. Let's read John 4:14. Sometimes the revelation is so deep that you cannot use your own words to explain it and God will reveal through the Word.

***But whosoever drinketh of the water that I shall give him shall never thirst; but the water that I shall give him shall be in him a well of water springing up into everlasting life.***

Now, what I am talking about in the prophetic utterance is that well of water. Some Christians have it, but they never tap into it. You see them. They are born again. They love Christ. They love God, but they are just shy people. They never tap into that well, and the well is meant to flow out. Some of these people just carry that well inside of them.

And they do not want to grow. For the water to come out, you must be determined to grow. How do I explain this? Lord, help me. Look at that woman that Jesus Christ met at the well, she uses the gift that she has negatively before. She was using it to marry men. She married like 5 of them. She knows how to talk to men. She knows how to whisper to them, even the one that she was sleeping with was not her husband. You know she is good at her game.

Now when she met with Christ, God now changes that well into a living water. She was coming to get natural water to fill that thirst, but now God opened up that well that has been locked up in her body for generations. So now when the well comes in contact with the owner, the owner is able to speak to the well. When he speaks to the well, he makes contact with Jesus Christ. The well that has been lying down there, that has never been used just pours out.

Now she was able to use that well to bring every man in the city to Jesus Christ. You know what? She has a choice not to open her mouth. That's why this thing about walking with God it's very, very deep. Because some people will still make a choice not to use that well until they die. Just like the man they gave one talent, he buried it. That was his choice not to use it. He had his own personal reasons why he doesn't want to use his talent. Same thing with us. I don't want to be a Pastor. You are saying all of those negative things. I am not called to teach. So you are killing yourself not to make the well burst out. So all that this does is seal up the well properly for you and it never comes out.

That is why it is so important for children of God to confess positive. As you are here, your calling is not news to God. You will discover your calling as you walk with God. God already knows your calling. You, discover it by obeying God. As you walk on the road of obedience, you will just see some things begin to open up to you. Now you begin to discover yourself.

Your anointing and your gift, is revealed to you as you walk with God. God knows who you are going to be. Remember what he told Jeremiah, before you are born I knew you already. I'm just letting you know who you are. Because he was walking in obedience, God spoke to him. If he was not walking in obedience, there would be no reason to call him Jeremiah. Do you see my point? Every road of obedience, leads to a call. Most of the time people are not patient enough to stay on that road long enough to discover who they are in Christ. They get frustrated. They get tired. They get weary. They look for excuses. "It's too long a journey. It's not enjoyable. It's not good." That's why you are called.

So prophetic utterance, is something that is up to you. Remember, Jesus did not have plans to stay in the Samaria for 3 days, it's is what that woman that made Jesus to do a revival there. That was not in the plan of Jesus. So whatever we do, is what makes room for God in our lives.

God has no problem blessing you. God has no problem making you Joyce Meyers or TD Jakes. It is your obedience that carries you to that level. It's not God's obedience, it is not God's willingness, it is your obedience that makes you to be who you are.

So the Word can be there but if you choose not to stretch yourself or not make any effort towards your spiritual life, the well be there forever and never be used or tapped in to. The gift will never be manifested. You will never be a blessing to anybody.

Praise the Lord. The master plan of God is wrapped up inside of you dormant until you come into contact with Jesus. Remember, that man that was possessed with 1000 demons. The original plan of God for him was to be an Evangelist. The moment he was delivered, the Bible says he went out into 10 cities. Can you imagine? 10 cities to share the gospel. That was the original plan of God for his life, but the enemy locked him down in a tomb cutting himself. That plan was always in him all he had to do is to come in contact with the Ancient of Days and the river would burst open. The real person will now come out.

It's like God peeling an onion as you walk with him. Many times people want to run ahead of God. You cannot run ahead of him. The training and discovery of who you are is on that road. The revelation of who you are will come on that road of obedience, but you have to be willing to walk on that road. People are not willing to walk on that road. God will never do anything without training you. He will never use anyone without training. He does not do that. He never does that. He didn't do that with his son. He will not excuse anybody.

Now, some people will just give you revelation and say this is what the Lord is saying. Now as a child of God, we must go to God and say where am I supposed to serve. What am I supposed to do? When we don't ask the right questions, we might not get the right answers for years.

Now when you ask the right questions, and you walk God, He will tell you. He said come unto me and I will answer you. He will tell you stay in this church. Do this and just stay there. He will give you answers. God is not a God that does not talk. God talks. When we ask the right questions he will give us the right answer. If you don't ask the right question you might go for years not knowing what to do or how to do it. When you ask the right question, we must be patient enough to listen to him. He may not talk to you in two months. He might not talk to you in 3 months. He might not talk to you in 4 months. Keep on saying Lord, this is really a burden for me I want to know. He will talk. He is not a wicked God. He will talk.

It depends on what side we are leaning on. That determines sometimes what you get from him. That's why He said I am that I am. I am to you what you believe that I am. If you don't believe that I can open the Red Sea, I will never open the Red Sea in your life.

We should be careful about what we are hearing and what everyone is prophesying to us. There are a lot of prophecies out there that people say and say. God help us. Amen.

That's why is good to teach instead of prophesying every Sunday because it doesn't grow people. Prophecy can make people feel good, " this is what is going to happen to you", but after that what is next.

How am I going to walk in that path? How am I going to receive that blessing? How am I going to get to that destination? You are saying that this is where I am going, how am I going to get there? That's why it is good to pray. Any prophetic word that anyone may tell you, if you don't pray with it, it may not even come to pass. You must pray. That's why Jesus Christ prayed very much to go to that cross. Prayer is what brings the promises of God to reality.

So no matter what anyone can tell you, even if you yourself don't pray on it, seriously, it might not work. It will be as if that man lied to you. He didn't lie; it's just that you are not serious enough to pursue what God has said. Remember, it is God that does things, but it is our job to pray ourselves into it. Promises of God can hang in the air for years and will not come to reality without prayer. Prayer is what bring promises to reality.

So no matter what anybody tells us, no matter whatever we hear we should go and pray on it except you don't want to be that person. If you really want to be that person and you feel in your spirit that what that person has said is for me, then you pray yourself into it. Meet with God and ask him to show you what to do consistently and to guide you. "I want to understand this prophecy". "Give me Revelation. Give me an example".

Pray on that prophecy every day until you get the thing in your hand. It now depends on how serious we take the word, how serious we accept the word. If that word makes any meaning to you, then you pray yourself into it.

There is no word that anybody can give us. You must have had that feeling about that something before. It should be a confirmation of what you have been feeling or have heard in the spirit or be in connection somewhere. So we must understand how these things work. The Lord will help us as we walk on this journey together. So prophetic utterance is something that is inside of you. Praise the Lord. Amen.

You have everything in you as a prophet. How do I know that? Let's look at John chapter 7:38

***38 He that believeth on me, as the scripture hath said, out of his belly shall flow rivers of living water.***

So there is something that is not flowing before until we believe. We must believe in who you are until the river flows. That woman was totally convinced that Jesus Christ had delivered her. That is why she had the boldness to invite all of those men to a revival. If she was not convinced, the river would never flow. The only way you can operate in your anointing is that you must believe in yourself. You must believe who you are and not that people are telling you who you are; you must know who you are. People have told me some things about myself, but it's not news to me I know who I am. You must have the confidence to flow in that grace, to flow in that anointing. If you are not sure of yourself, you will never flow in it.

The Bible says he that believes in me, you must believe what He has said about you. You must believe what the Bible says you are. You must believe you have the gift. You must believe you have the anointing. As the scripture has said, then out of your belly shall flow living water. What is living water? You are blessing people. You are changing dry bones to life. This is why this anointing has such a powerful concern for me. The strangest part of this is that you as a prophet you may not be received. People may not be receptive of what you are saying. Jesus was not received in Nazareth, but that does not make Him not know who He is. He still operated somewhere else.

Can you imagine if no one ask for me to pray for them anymore in the ministry for whatever reason, God will still use me somewhere else. It makes no difference. If no one calls me for prayer anymore, it does not reduce my anointing because I know who I am.

The fact that some people may not receive you or submit to you, does not mean that it makes you less than who you are. You must have that confidence. So as your spirit communicates via your emotions through your urim and thummin, so also the spirit communicates through your dreams and visions, and so your spirit communicate via your will which is your speech or your utterance that is will power. You must believe in who you are and what God has called you to be and what He has chosen you to do, the water will flow.

One thing that is wonderful about this prophetic utterance is that as a child of God you must develop yourself in speaking in tongues. In speaking in tongues, you are able to discover more and more of your grace. In speaking in tongues, you are able to develop boldness. In speaking in tongues, you are able to develop your self-portrait and self-esteem. So, even when you are rejected, it does not reduce who you are. You don't suffer from low self-esteem because someone said they didn't like you. Your self-portrait is intact because you pray in the Holy Spirit. It doesn't matter how anyone treat you because you are okay. You know the anointing is there. You know the well is there.

One thing about speaking in tongues is that it helps you to operate and prophecy better. When you are speaking in tongues, you are speaking in the language of angels. You are speaking in the language given to you by the Spirit. You quickly go into the will of God when you speak in tongues and you are able to draw facts from the will of God and connect to your will and declare what the Lord is saying according to Romans 12:2.

***[2]And be not conformed to this world: but be ye transformed by the renewing of your mind, that ye may prove what is that good, and acceptable, and perfect, will of God.***

When speaking in tongues you are able to draw from the will of God quicker. If you don't speak in tongues, you will have to work on your will. You must have trained you will to submit to the will of God to be able to speak boldly and be sure it is God speaking. If you are not speaking in tongues, it will take time maybe through worship or prayer before you can get the will of God out. If you are speaking in tongues, it is easier for you to go into the spirit and bring the will of God into the physical into that situation.

Sometimes when God is interested in your destiny, He will force His will upon you as in the case of Jonah. You know Jonah did not want to do the will of God. Jonah would have preferred to just mind his own business. It was God that compelled him to deliver that message. So, if God has positioned you in a very vital part in the kingdom of God and your assignment is needed in the Kingdom, God will compel you to do His will which we see that He has done several times. Tell me the truth do you think Paul really wanted to become born again? Paul was not planning on becoming born again. It was Jesus that met him. Paul did not know what it meant to be born again. It was not in his plan. So sometimes if you are vital to the assignment of the Kingdom, He will compel you and at that point you will not have any excuse.

He will compel you and hold you down. Some people say that

God does not force people. They are making a big mistake except you are not important. If you are important, He will make you. He made Paul and He can make anyone else. God is a sovereign. God can do whatever he likes. No one can question Him. No one can say totally this is not God, He doesn't do things like that. You are lying because you are not sure. Just because He hasn't done it doesn't mean He can't do it.

I will never say anything total about God because God is able to do anything. That is the way I operate my life. That's why I believe in him so much. That's why I experienced his miracles so much. I believe He can do anything and He does that in my life again and again and again. Don't ever, people of God, don't ever limit God. Don't ever say God cannot do that.

God will sometimes use angels. It's not because He doesn't believe in you or I as His children to perform His assignments, but He will use angels to carry out his assignment especially when it is very urgent. When it is very urgent, God will send an angel right from the throne of grace to deliver a message to you immediately. He will not wait for any man to say it. He will not wait for any person to tell you. He will not wait for any Prophet to tell you. It will just come directly from an angel. Let's look at Acts chapter 27:23.

***23 For there stood by me this night the angel of God, whose I am, and whom I serve,***

So sometimes God will not wait to minister to you because it will be too late. He would just send an angel. Those angels are powerful. They can move with speed of light. Once God lift his finger, they will appear in that situation or circumstance immediately and they perform. I love Angels because they are ministers to us. Ministers to our destiny. They protect us. They care for us. They make a way for us.

For example I was driving about 30 miles per hour and a guy

in front of me came to a complete stop. The road was wet and honestly I don't know what stopped my car. Normally when you press your brakes under these circumstances, your car will skid. Fortunately for me, my car did not skid. I press my brakes and the car just stopped. Even my wife was amazed. We would have ran into the back of that car. It could have been an angel that just stood there. That's why I love angels. They come and protect you. They come and deliver you. They come and do strange things in your life. If you have a mind of God, you will know that some of the things that happen to you and I, is by seconds or minutes is the act of an Angel. They just come there and either delay you and the accident happened before you got there or you just pass there and an accident happened.

So why do we hear Angels by the reason of their message. Sometimes we cannot make direct impression our own mind, the Angels appearance makes direct impression on your mind. You have no doubt that you have seen an angel and so that changes everything. That changes your position. Sometimes it comes as confirmation. Sometimes they come as a decree or declaration from God. We see how Angels work with prophets. We see how Angels worked with Daniel several times. Praise the Lord.

5. Hearing God through self-development. You hear God because you have been studying, you have been praying, you have been seeking God, you have been hungry for God, and you will see yourself hearing God more and more audibly. Let us look at Habakkuk 2:1

***1 I will stand upon my watch, and set me upon the tower, and will watch to see what he will say unto me, and what I shall answer when I am reproved.***

That means an effort has been made. You sit down in your house because maybe you are off that day and you say "today God speak to me. I want to hear God about my situation. God, I need you to speak." You have trained yourself to hear from God. You have made up your mind that you are not moving an inch until God speaks and if he does not speak that day then the next day when you are off you wait for the Lord.

The scripture says that I will wait upon a tower, that means you find a place that is quiet and where you will not be disturbed by any noise or your private room where you pray. Your mind is made up. It is a determination of seeking God. You are resolute and you make time for that Word every day. You know God is a good God. When you make up your mind like that He will always fulfill it.

# CHAPTER 6

# DUTIES AS A PROPHET

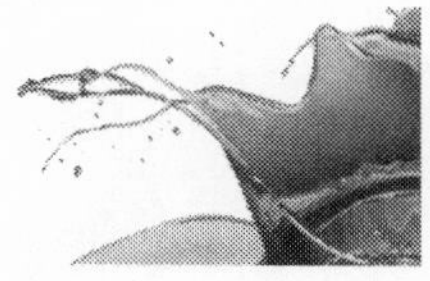

In the book of Ezekiel 33:7,

***[7]So thou, O son of man, I have set thee a watchman unto the house of Israel; therefore thou shalt hear the word at my mouth, and warn them from me.***

That is your assignment as a prophet.

Ez. 33:8-20

***[8] When I say unto the wicked, O wicked man, thou shalt surely die; if thou dost not speak to warn the wicked from his way, that wicked man shall die in his iniquity; but his blood will I require at thine hand.[9] Nevertheless, if thou warn the wicked of his way to turn from it; if he do not turn from his way, he shall die in his iniquity; but thou hast delivered thy soul.[10] Therefore, O thou son of man, speak unto the house of Israel; Thus ye speak, saying, If our transgressions and our sins be upon us, and we pine away in them, how should we then live?[11] Say unto them, As I live, saith the Lord GOD, I have no pleasure in the death of the wicked; but that the wicked turn from his way and live: turn ye, turn ye from your evil ways; for why will ye die, O house of Israel?***

***12 Therefore, thou son of man, say unto the children of thy people, The righteousness of the righteous shall not deliver him in the day of his transgression: as for the wickedness of the wicked, he shall not fall thereby in the day that he turneth from his wickedness; neither shall the righteous be able to live for his righteousness in the day that he sinneth. 13 When I shall say to the righteous, that he shall surely live; if he trust to his own righteousness, and commit iniquity, all his righteousnesses shall not be remembered; but for his iniquity that he hath committed, he shall die for it. 14 Again, when I say unto the wicked, Thou shalt surely die; if he turn from his sin, and do that which is lawful and right;***

***15 If the wicked restore the pledge, give again that he had robbed, walk in the statutes of life, without committing iniquity; he shall surely live, he shall not die. 16 None of his sins that he hath committed shall be mentioned unto him: he hath done that which is lawful and right; he shall surely live. 17 Yet the children of thy people say, The way of the Lord is not equal: but as for them, their way is not equal.***

***18 When the righteous turneth from his righteousness, and committeth iniquity, he shall even die thereby. 19 But if the wicked turn from his wickedness, and do that which is lawful and right, he shall live thereby. 20 Yet ye say, The way of the Lord is not equal. O ye house of Israel, I will judge you every one after his ways.***

You know these type of messages are not preached in the church anymore. People may become afraid and not come to church anymore. Instead of running to God they would just run away, but that's the honest truth. This is why we need to wake up as children of God. The Lord will help us in the name of Jesus. So this is your position. Your job is to build the church.

If you notice, the Bible kept saying the house of Israel. Unbelievers is not your assignment, it is the body of Christ. To build them up, to warn them of their wicked ways, so that they will turn back to God and be restored.

God said if I tell you to tell somebody about their unrighteousness and his wickedness, and you refused to tell him, his blood will be required from your hand. If you tell him and he did not change his ways, you are no longer guilty. That person will die for his sins and his blood will be on his own head. So you must remember that you are a Watchman.

That's why your position is very important. I want us to look at some strange instructions. One thing I want us to know about God is when he calls you as a prophet, every detail of your life is prepared.

Where you go, where you go to school, the life you are living, the person you marry, your job, every detail of your life is prepared by God. This is not to say that every other Christian does not enjoy this but, yours is different. Why yours is different is because every detail of your life is not only ordered by God but it is prophetic. Again this is not to say that the lives of every other Christian is not ordered by God because the Bible clearly states that the steps of the righteous are ordered by the Lord, but your life is prophetic.

Everything you are doing is prophetic. The losing of your job, your going home, your dying, your living, your walk, -it is prepared. You cannot take anything for granted. Let me give you some examples. Jonah 1:17

***[17] Now the LORD had prepared a great fish to swallow up Jonah. And Jonah was in the belly of the fish three days and three nights.***

Can you imagine? Someone jumps in the water and want to die, in the Bible record that the Lord prepared a big fish. A big fish that does not have a soul that is responding to God.

Jonah was in the belly of the fish three days and three nights which also signifies a prophetic move of what will happen to Jesus Christ. So that means the death of Jesus Christ was prepared. You prepare the enemy to swallow his soul up. Three days and three nights that was the three days three nights that Jesus was in the grave.

So, we must understand the importance. Let's go to the book of Jonah Chapter 4:6

***[6] And the LORD God prepared a gourd, and made it to come up over Jonah, that it might be a shadow over his head, to deliver him from his grief. So Jonah was exceeding glad of the gourd.***

This God is amazing. A plant that we sow into the ground, God just make it grow up overnight. God prepared a plant to be a shade over Jonah. Why is God doing all these things? He wants to reveal something to Jonah. That's how powerful God is. He will use anything that you are going through in your life to send a message to you. Every detail of your life is important. Let's look at Jonah 4 v 7.

***[7] But God prepared a worm when the morning rose the next day, and it smote the gourd that it withered***

Do we know what a worm is? A worm is something that eats plants. Worm that we don't even know can respond to its Maker, will not respond to you, but will respond to God. So what God is telling us through this information is that every detail of your life no matter how minute is important. Do you know how small a worm is? God had time to prepare a worm all because He had a message to send to somebody. He will do the same thing in your life. That's why we have to pay attention to every detail of our lives. Let's look at Jonah 4:8.

***8 And it came to pass, when the sun did arise, that God prepared a vehement east wind; and the sun beat upon the head of Jonah, that he fainted, and wished in himself to die, and said, It is better for me to die than to live.***

God prepared another thing again. God prepared a wind. So, you are going out as a prophet and the wind is already prepared by God to speak something to you. One day I was driving from the Northside of Houston to the Southwest side of Houston and I entered Beltway 8. I entered this rain on Beltway 8. Terrible rain. People were parking on the side and my windshield wiper was not moving fast enough. It was so dark. I have never seen that type of rain before. The cloud was almost touching the ground. The cloud was so heavy. Dark clouds. The visibility was zero. I had to reduce my speed to 10 miles per hour. I wanted to panic and the Spirit of God told me not to panic but go through it. "When you park, the storm stays on top of you. You go through it. Even when you are crawling, keep on going."

So, I obeyed even though it was difficult. I was driving so slow. That was the slowest I have ever driven in this country. As I was edging forward, the next thing I saw was light ahead. My goodness! My spirit jumped in me. I was so excited. Even though I was still in the storm, I knew that I would soon be coming out. I continued to inch towards the light and I thought this God is fearful. By the time I drove a little longer on the road, I came into solid and bright sky. That was the day I feared God more. Not that I didn't fear Him before, but this day I feared the Lord. As I looked back in my rearview mirror, people were still in that storm. It was still raining so heavily. People were still parked thinking that the storm was all over Houston not knowing that it was clear just ahead of them. I say, my goodness.

I said, "Holy Spirit, thank You for encouraging me to keep on moving." So, it is amazing how God will use anything to teach big lessons. That is one of the reasons why I'm holding on in this ministry because I remember vividly what I went through on that day. Storm. Blinding storm. It was a lesson I will never forget. Even as I am sharing it with you, I can still see the rain. The rain was so heavy. I will never forget the message inflicted on my heart. This is what helps me to hold on no matter how bad it may look because there is always an end to every storm. Always.

So, now let's read some strange instructions because as God's prophet, I want to prepare your mind of what you can expect as a prophet. If you don't know then you won't know how to handle the word of God that you are hearing. You will not know when God is speaking to you when it looks as if it doesn't make sense. Let's read some things that will shock you. Mark it in your bible. 1 Kings 20:35-43

***35 And a certain man of the sons of the prophets said unto his neighbour in the word of the LORD, Smite me, I pray thee. And the man refused to smite him.***

***36** **Then said he unto him, Because thou hast not obeyed the***
***voice of the LORD, behold, as soon as thou art departed from***
***me, a lion shall slay thee. And as soon as he was departed***
***from him, a lion found him, and slew him. 37 Then he found***
***another man, and said, Smite me, I pray thee. And the man***
***smote him, so that in smiting he wounded him. 38 So the***
***prophet departed, and waited for the king by the way, and***
***disguised himself with ashes upon his face.***

***39 And as the king passed by, he cried unto the king: and he***
***said, Thy servant went out into the midst of the battle; and,***
***behold, a man turned aside, and brought a man unto me, and***
***said, Keep this man: if by any means he be missing, then***
***shall thy life be for his life, or else thou shalt pay a talent of***
***silver. 40 And as thy servant was busy here and there, he was***
***gone. And the king of Israel said unto him, So shall thy***
***judgment be; thyself hast decided it.***

***41 And he hasted, and took the ashes away from his face; and***
***the king of Israel discerned him that he was of the prophets.***
***42 And he said unto him, Thus saith the LORD, Because thou***
***hast let go out of thy hand a man whom I appointed to utter***
***destruction, therefore thy life shall go for his life, and thy***
***people for his people. 43 And the king of Israel went to his***
***house heavy and displeased, and came to Samaria.***

So, the school of prophecy has always existed in the bible. We see in scripture where it says, "sons of prophet." There were in a school like you are in a class. Praise the Lord. They were being trained by a prophet. So, we see when you disobey a prophetic word over your life, you are actually disobeying God.

Can you imagine, a prophet is saying to someone to wound him so that he may deliver a message from God. That is your job. He will make your life a message to people. Whatever you are going through will be a message to people, and if you understand who you are, when challenges of life come, ask the Lord, "Daddy, what are you trying to teach everybody else?". Not you. Remember, He uses your life. You are an instrument. He reserves the right to do anything to you. It's not easy for someone to say, "stab me on the side"? That's why the first man could not, and he judged the person that was afraid to stab him. He called somebody else, "wound me." That person obeyed. He wounded him and he's bleeding. The prophet put ashes on his face and went and sat by the roadside to wait for the king. Remember, God told him to deliver a message. Can you believe that?

This prophetic assignment is interesting because God will be doing things in your life and the things He will be asking you to do will not be normal to people. This is still in the bible. This is not something outside of the bible. We have read it together.

I will use a lot of examples so that you will understand that you are so precious to God. So, the things that He will be doing through you in your life is a depiction of the heart of God towards His people. So we have here a king that disobeyed God and God was displeased with that king. Since God could not come down and display that action of wounding Himself, He chooses His prophet to do it. Can you imagine the pain to stab yourself or have someone else to stab you? The pain just to deliver a message from God.

Let's read 2 Samuel 12:1-7.

***And the LORD sent Nathan unto David. And he came unto
him, and said unto him, There were two men in one city; the
one rich, and the other poor. 2 The rich man had exceeding
many flocks and herds: 3 But the poor man had nothing, save
one little ewe lamb, which he had bought and nourished up:
and it grew up together with him, and with his children; it did
eat of his own meat, and drank of his own cup, and lay in his
bosom, and was unto him as a daughter.***

***4 And there came a traveler unto the rich man, and he spared
to take of his own flock and of his own herd, to dress for the
wayfaring man that was come unto him; but took the poor
man's lamb, and dressed it for the man that was come to him.***

***5 And David's anger was greatly kindled against the man; and
he said to Nathan, As the LORD liveth, the man that hath
done this thing shall surely die: 6 And he shall restore the
lamb fourfold, because he did this thing, and because he had
no pity. 7 And Nathan said to David, Thou art the man. Thus
saith the LORD God of Israel, I anointed thee king over Israel,
and I delivered thee out of the hand of Saul;***

Can you face the president of a nation or a king or your husband or wife or even your Pastor and give them a parable like this? That takes a lot of boldness. You know that right? These are the things that God can give you as an instructions to go and do. You cannot say, "God, the king?" Remember, no one dares open their mouths against the king. In the Old Testament, even today, you dare not go against the king or president.

People should be fearful of talking anyhow to a Pastor that

God has sent to your life. You understand? That person is not accountable to you, they are accountable to God, except you have a message like Nathan and you know that God sent you. You better be sure because if you are wrong like Miriam and Aaron, then you are in trouble.

That person will not have to say anything to you. God will just arise and fight on their behalf. When God arises and fights on behalf of that man/woman, you don't want to see that fight.

Let's look at Isaiah 20:1-3

***[1]In the year that Tartan came unto Ashdod, (when Sargon the king of Assyria sent him,) and fought against Ashdod, and took it; [2] At the same time spake the LORD by Isaiah the son of Amoz, saying, Go and loose the sackcloth from off thy loins, and put off thy shoe from thy foot. And he did so, walking naked and barefoot. [3] And the LORD said, Like as my servant Isaiah hath walked naked and barefoot three years for a sign and wonder upon Egypt and upon Ethiopia;***

Can you imagine, walking naked for three years to obey God. If any man of God does that today, people would finish him totally. People would lock him up never to see the light of the day, talking about God. Nobody preaches this about Isaiah. We talk about good things about Isaiah, but his anointing came with suffering. He suffered for that anointing. That's why he had those powerful revelations. At this point, Isaiah is not talking about the anointing of God, how God will give you the hidden treasures of His heart. He has not talked about those things at this time. His obedience brought about revelation. That's why from Isaiah chapter 35 forward is so wonderful and powerful with revelation, giving deep insight into the arrival of Jesus Christ and what God is planning to do for His children at the end of time. Who would believe that God would ask a man to do this? This is not preached about Isaiah. Nobody preaches this about Isaiah. He walked naked for 3 ½ years.

We all quote, "they that wait upon the Lord…" . It's easy to quote, but look at what he did. The Bible says in Hebrews 13:8,

***8 Jesus Christ the same yesterday, and to day, and for ever.***

So, if God can do these things then, why can't He do those things now? He may not do it in that level of nakedness. He might strip you of your job. He may strip you of your money. You are broke and don't even know what is happening to you. Most of the time, what we will say is that it is "the enemy attacking me".

This nakedness might be spiritual dryness to just give a message to somebody. Let me tell you what the Lord did with me. I was just eating. I was just craving for food. In one hour, I was hungry again. I had to sit myself down and ask what was wrong with me. Then the Lord said to me, "that is how it is when someone is living in sin". They crave for it and can't control themselves." I said, "Daddy, is that why you are making me eat like this?" My wife is my witness. I had to sit my wife down and ask her if there was anything wrong with me.

I don't like food like this. I mean what was going on? Just stuffing myself, but He will use things in your life. One thing is that when you are going through things that are strange and you cannot understand, what helps is to quickly go back to God. Ask Him, "Daddy, what's going on?" "Why am I going through this?"

If you don't ask questions, you can be in that position and lose your mind if you are not careful. So, we must understand how God does these things. It is so deep. That's why I gave you this example now before we go to the good part, symbols and dreams. Those are the good parts. I'm trying to tell you the instructions that God can give you now so that you can sit down and think very well.

You must know what you are trying to enter in to. I cannot deceive you. I will not lie to you. If I make it look so good that you will prophecy to nations. It comes with a price. "You are going to be used by God," but it comes with a price.

People of God, I don't want to boast about attacks that I go through in my house that God has delivered me and my wife from. To be a Pastor of this ministry, I have been through some things. I don't want to be coming to church talking about those things because everybody else is going through something. So if Pastor is shouting about devil every day, everyone will leave the church.

If I come on the pulpit talking about what I saw yesterday, you come to Bible study and I tell you what the devil did today, people will start to say, "maybe we are in the wrong church". One thing I want you to understand is that the devil likes to show off. Don't ever magnify what he does. You will give him a good footing in your life. Ignore him.

When you ignore him, you have the victory. When you ignore him, he will say, "this one is a crazy Christian. Let me just leave him alone because he doesn't even pay me any attention". If you begin to talk about what you are going through, you have given him the upper hand in your life. Just like Joseph, prison in a king's palace is not going down, it's actually going up. It may physically look like a prison. Sometimes the ways of God are so strange. You cannot explain them, except He gives you an insight. If people that are walking with you are not sure of what God is saying to you, they might get weary.

Let's go to Isaiah 38:1

***[1]In those days was Hezekiah sick unto death. And Isaiah the prophet the son of Amoz came unto him, and said unto him, Thus saith the LORD, Set thine house in order: for thou shalt die, and not live.***

How can you go to somebody house and say this instead of you to pray for that person. Just tell him to set his house in order. You see Pastor coming into your house and you are in your bed and you are so happy to see Pastor. Praising God that Pastor has finally come, and he gets in there and says, "Brother, get your house in order. I am so sorry. The Lord said, your sickness is unto death."

Tell me now, who do you want to deliver that message to that will not use his last strength to slap you?! "At least if I am going to die, let me slap you first. At least I will go to Heaven slapping you."

Now, you deliver the message. Let's assume that they respect you and smack their lips and say under their breath, "useless Pastor" and walk you out and say goodbye, and as you are going out, it says, Isaiah ch. 38:2-3 (He didn't even answer the man of God, he respected and honored him and he knows that it is God's business, and it's not him-referring to the prophet)

***[2] Then Hezekiah turned his face toward the wall, and prayed unto the LORD, [3] And said, Remember now, O LORD, I beseech thee, how I have walked before thee in truth and with***

***a perfect heart, and have done that which is good in thy sight. And Hezekiah wept sore.***

That's why as children of God, we must be faithful. As a prophet, have a spiritual account that you can use to address God in case anything comes up in your life that God can use as a point of contact to remember you. People of God, God is merciful. Where was I going to get money to buy another car when my car got burned? All the little change we get comes to the ministry first. House of David is our priority. I pray for all of you to have savings, but I don't have a savings account. All of my money comes to the ministry. So where do I go? God knew that and He made a way. Because God knew the insurance would not pay for it all, He made a way for someone to give me a car. Now, the devil is regretting what he did.

The Bible records that if the prince of this world had knew. The devil is regretting now because if he knew what he had done to us would cause me to come out of a car note, he wouldn't have done it. Now, he did what he did and I have another car, no car note, a better car, a newer car, rides better, than the one I was driving.

My wife's car that was also burned partially, her car was fixed and it is better, looks more beautiful. The car we were postponing to paint, is painted. The headlights changed. Our fence that was breaking down that animals were coming under to poop in my yard, has been fixed and done better. So if the devil knew that this would have made our lives better, you think he would have attacked? No.

The devil doesn't know everything. So, he prayed and look at what happened, Isaiah 38:4-5

***4 Then came the word of the LORD to Isaiah, saying, 5 Go, and say to Hezekiah, Thus saith the LORD, the God of David thy father, I have heard thy prayer, I have seen thy tears: behold, I will add unto thy days fifteen years.***

This is where your job is difficult. Now, you are going and they smacked their lips at you the first time. You carried your shame. Remember, you are not responsible for the response of the people with the word of God. You are a messenger. Whether they slap you or they kick you, it is none of your business. He sent you. You deliver the message.

So, he was going, taking his shame, and God spoke to him again. "Isaiah, go back to that house where they just shamed you or ignored you and tell him that I saw his prayer and I'm going to bless him."

Funny enough, they opened the door for him which is not normal. In this world today, when they sent you out of the house like that, you are not entering that house again. Once they see you coming back, they will shout "close the door!" They wouldn't even want to hear what the prophet has to say. That is where a lot of people miss it. That is where millions have missed it. Not only prophetic officers and generals, but even the receiver. The receiver too was hurt by the first message of what the man of God said to the person, and they get angry and leave. Now when God sends the right word of God to them because they have left, they missed it. Sometimes even the prophet does not want to deliver the message.

"Lord, you told me this person was going to die, now you want me to tell him something different? No, I won't tell him." This is where your work is difficult. You are an instrument. He can send you with a message of death and send you back to the same person with a message of life. You cannot be emotionally involved. You cannot think that the person deserved judgement. It's none of your business. You are an instrument. He commands you. You obey. He instructs. You carry out His will. You have no feeling. You have no opinion. You have no suggestion. You have no input. It is your assignment. Just do His will. John 6:38 which says

***[38] For I came down from heaven, not to do mine own will, but the will of him that sent me.***

Whichever way He wants to do with His creature, it is none of your business. Praise the Lord. Hallelujah.

# CHAPTER 7

# STRANGE INSTRUCTIONS AS A PROPHET

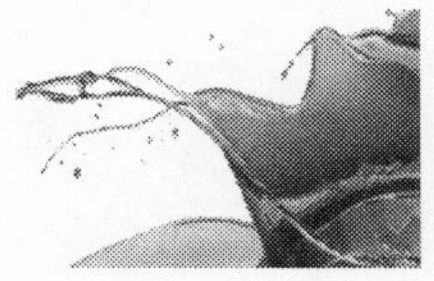

Let's read Jeremiah chapter 16:1-2.

***[1]The word of the Lord came also unto me, saying, [2] Thou shalt not take thee a wife, neither shalt thou have sons or daughters in this place.***

Is that an easy commandment? I don't think so. God is telling a prophet that "you cannot marry". It is an instruction that must be carried out. There is no negotiation. You know each time the word of the Lord came to somebody, in the book of John, it is Jesus. So anytime anyone says that Jesus was not introduced in the Old Testament is a liar. The word is not physical. It is spiritual. It says the word of the Lord came.

What they are trying to do is to make you understand that this Word has personality. In other words, it is a person. So Jeremiah was given an instruction. Let's look at chapter 16:3-4.

***[3]For thus saith the Lord concerning the sons and concerning the daughters that are born in this place, and concerning their mothers that bare them, and concerning their fathers that begat them in this land; [4]They shall die of grievous deaths; they shall not be lamented; neither shall they be buried; but they shall be as dung upon the face of the earth: and they shall be consumed by the sword, and by famine; and their***

***carcasses shall be meat for the fowls of heaven, and for the beasts of the earth***

So if God would have just told Jeremiah part A, Jeremiah would have thought that this was not good for a man of God. Look at why. Look at the reason why God is giving him that instruction. As a prophet, when God is giving you an utterance or giving you a word, the advantage and disadvantage of the word will be clearly identified to you.

So you are looking at a serious issue here. God is saying to the man of God I know that these people are beautiful but evil. You don't know how many churches are beautiful, everything perfect, beautiful musicians, 20 member choir, but God says all of them will die like a dog. God says that He's not with them and that they are useless.

God had to give him that instruction because the country must have looked so nice physically. God was trying to make him see His position on something that looks so beautiful. God was telling Jeremiah not to get involved. So we must understand how these things can be with God when He is using you as his prophet.

He will give you strange instructions, but He will also tell you why. Don't listen to half of a message and run. Just like we read verses 1 & 2 and thought Oh my goodness, how can God do this to a man of God? But when you read the rest of it did you not change your mind? So that is the thing. God says I'm going to do this for this sister. Don't just jump up and tell the sister anything. Let God finish what He is saying. Let God finish the message. When you want to say something, He will give you a complete sentence that cannot be questioned. So that anyone that is listening to you will know that it makes sense what you are saying. It will be confirmed in their spirit.

Let's go to another example. Let's read Jeremiah 32:1-9.

***1 The word that came to Jeremiah from the Lord in the tenth year of Zedekiah king of Judah, which was the eighteenth year of Nebuchadrezzar. 2 For then the king of Babylon's army besieged Jerusalem: and Jeremiah the prophet was shut up in the court of the prison, which was in the king of Judah's house. 3 For Zedekiah king of Judah had shut him up, saying, Wherefore dost thou prophesy, and say, Thus saith the Lord, Behold, I will give this city into the hand of the king of Babylon, and he shall take it; 4 And Zedekiah king of Judah shall not escape out of the hand of the Chaldeans, but shall surely be delivered into the hand of the king of Babylon, and shall speak with him mouth to mouth, and his eyes shall behold his eyes; 5 And he shall lead Zedekiah to Babylon, and there shall he be until I visit him, saith the Lord: though ye fight with the Chaldeans, ye shall not prosper. 6 And Jeremiah said, The word of the Lord came unto me, saying, 7 Behold, Hanameel the son of Shallum thine uncle shall come unto thee saying, Buy thee my field that is in Anathoth: for the right of redemption is thine to buy it. 8 So Hanameel mine uncle's son came to me in the court of the prison according to the word of the Lord, and said unto me, Buy my field, I pray thee, that is in Anathoth, which is in the country of Benjamin: for the right of inheritance is thine, and the redemption is thine; buy it for thyself. Then I knew that this was the word of the Lord. 9 And I bought the field of Hanameel my uncle's son, that was in Anathoth, and weighed him the money, even seventeen shekels of silver.***

Let's continue starting at verse 14.

***14 Thus saith the Lord of hosts, the God of Israel; Take these***

***evidences, this evidence of the purchase, both which is sealed, and this evidence which is open; and put them in an earthen vessel, that they may continue many days.***

This is how God operates. He will use your life and give you instructions that will benefit you and bless others.

Let's look at Ezekiel chapter 16:16-21.

16***And of thy garments thou didst take, and deckedst thy high***
***places with divers colours, and playedst the harlot thereupon:***
***the like things shall not come, neither shall it be so.*** 17***Thou***
***hast also taken thy fair jewels of my gold and of my silver,***
***which I had given thee, and madest to thyself images of men,***
***and didst commit whoredom with them,*** 18***And tookest thy***
***broidered garments, and coveredst them: and thou hast set***
***mine oil and mine incense before them.*** 19***My meat also which***
***I gave thee, fine flour, and oil, and honey, wherewith I fed***
***thee, thou hast even set it before them for a sweet savour: and***
***thus it was, saith the Lord God.*** 20***Moreover thou hast taken***
***thy sons and thy daughters, whom thou hast borne unto me,***
***and these hast thou sacrificed unto them to be devoured. Is***
***this of thy whoredoms a small matter,*** 21***That thou hast slain***
***my children, and delivered them to cause them to pass***
***through the fire for them?***

I want you to remember that they keep saying that the word of the Lord came. The word of the Lord is not a human being in the Old Testament as we understood it. We that have revelation of who Jesus was, we know that they are talking about Jesus. I want you to see that God is now telling the man of God that as a prophet he is a Watchman.

Let's read another example. Let's read Ezekiel Chapter 3:22-27

***22 And the hand of the Lord was there upon me; and he said***
***unto me, Arise, go forth into the plain, and I will there talk***
***with thee. 23 Then I arose, and went forth into the plain: and,***
***behold, the glory of the Lord stood there, as the glory which I***
***saw by the river of Chebar: and I fell on my face. 24 Then the***
***spirit entered into me, and set me upon my feet, and spake***
***with me, and said unto me, Go, shut thyself within thine***
***house. 25 But thou, O son of man, behold, they shall put bands***
***upon thee, and shall bind thee with them, and thou shalt not***
***go out among them: 26 And I will make thy tongue cleave to***
***the roof of thy mouth, that thou shalt be dumb, and shalt not***
***be to them a reprover: for they are a rebellious house. 27 But***
***when I speak with thee, I will open thy mouth, and thou shalt***
***say unto them, Thus saith the Lord God; He that heareth, let***
***him hear; and he that forbeareth, let him forbear: for they are***
***a rebellious house.***

Can you imagine? This is the first part. God wants to use this as an example to show the prophet what he must do. First of all, God will make the prophet dumb for days so that he can keep quiet and listen to God. After God has done that for days, then He tells the prophet to shut himself in the house and tie himself as if he is a prisoner. After God uses the prophet as an example to the people, then God will allow him to speak the message.

Now let us look at Ezekiel Chapter 4:4-6

***4 Lie thou also upon thy left side, and lay the iniquity of the***
***house of Israel upon it: according to the number of the days***
***that thou shalt lie upon it thou shalt bear their iniquity. 5 For I***
***have laid upon thee the years of their iniquity, according to***
***the number of the days, three hundred and ninety days: so***
***shalt thou bear the iniquity of the house of Israel. 6 And when***

***thou hast accomplished them, lie again on thy right side, and thou shalt bear the iniquity of the house of Judah forty days: I have appointed thee each day for a year.***

Lie on the ground on one side for 390 days. When you finished that side, you will turn to the other side and lie on the other side for 40 days. So you can see why God uses certain people to write these things. So you see how powerful you are to God. How important you are that God wants to use you to deliver the message, and He reserves the right to ask you to do anything to get the message across.

Let's read verse 12 in the same chapter. Ezekiel Chapter 4 :11-15

***11 Thou shalt drink also water by measure, the sixth part of an hin: from time to time shalt thou drink. 12 And thou shalt eat it as barley cakes, and thou shalt bake it with dung that cometh out of man, in their sight. 13 And the Lord said, Even thus shall the children of Israel eat their defiled bread among the Gentiles, whither I will drive them. 14 Then said I, Ah Lord God! behold, my soul hath not been polluted: for from my youth up even till now have I not eaten of that which dieth of itself, or is torn in pieces; neither came there abominable flesh into my mouth. 15 Then he said unto me, Lo, I have given thee cow's dung for man's dung, and thou shalt prepare thy bread therewith.***

Do you know what dung is? It is waste from men. God said you will mix human waste with flour, bake it, and eat it. Then after Ezekiel makes a comment about it, God then says, not to use man's waste but a cow's waste. People of God, that is God. If you continue in this book, you will see how God gave strange instructions. You won't believe how God will instruct His prophets.

Let's look at Ezekiel chapter 24:15-18

***15 Also the word of the Lord came unto me, saying, 16 Son of man, behold, I take away from thee the desire of thine eyes with a stroke: yet neither shalt thou mourn nor weep, neither shall thy tears run down. 17 Forbear to cry, make no mourning for the dead, bind the tire of thine head upon thee, and put on thy shoes upon thy feet, and cover not thy lips, and eat not the bread of men. 18 So I spake unto the people in the morning: and at even my wife died; and I did in the morning as I was commanded.***

God says, "man of God, I want to show you these people their evil ways and I will use you as an example." God takes his wife and tells him that he must not cry nor weep just wear his shoes and preach. If this was to happen today, how many people would understand that? So if God can do that to these people, then why not you?

Let's look at the book of Hosea Chapter 3:1-5

***1 Then said the Lord unto me, Go yet, love a woman beloved of her friend, yet an adulteress, according to the love of the Lord toward the children of Israel, who look to other gods, and love flagons of wine. 2 So I bought her to me for fifteen pieces of silver, and for an homer of barley, and an half homer of barley: 3 And I said unto her, Thou shalt abide for me many days; thou shalt not play the harlot, and thou shalt not be for another man: so will I also be for thee. 4 For the children of Israel shall abide many days without a king, and without a prince, and without a sacrifice, and without an image, and without an ephod, and without teraphim: 5 Afterward shall the children of Israel return, and seek the Lord their God, and David their king; and shall fear the Lord and his goodness in***

***the latter days.***

Can you imagine? God says that the prophet should marry an adulteress. So today, God may not tell you to go and buy a prostitute, but He can still give you strange instructions. Be sure that it is God. Don't go and do something crazy. These examples were given to you to understand how strange instructions can be for you as a prophet and how your obedience is equally important.

# CHAPTER 8
# DELIVERING THE MESSAGE AS A PROPHET

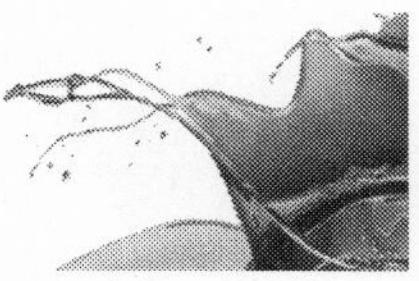

One of the biggest challenges in delivering the Word of God is our character traits. The problem is not in hearing, but delivering the message is the most difficult aspect of it. In delivering the message, we must consider timing. Timing of delivery is important. Timing is important because when you want to deliver the message, we must not deliver it at the wrong time. You can deliver the right message at the wrong time. You can do things right at the wrong time. As a prophet, your timing must be accurate. Look at the example of Esther.

How many of us knew that Esther was a prophet? Esther was used in that season as a prophet. Anybody that can stand in the gap for a nation is a prophet. She said "if I perish, I perish". How many people can do that? It's only prophet anointing that can take you to that point. A prophet is ready to lay his life down for a nation. A prophet is ready to stand in the gap for a whole nation.

He doesn't care what it will cost him. You don't have a life. You don't have your own life actually. You are a prophet. You are an instrument completely taken over by God. Not many people can live that life because at every stage, you finish one exam and you go into the next. God does not leave you alone. No breathing space. He's trying to squeeze everything that He can out of you to make you a sincere and transparent prophet for Him.

Some prophets have been dropped by God because of their disobedience. Because of their fleshy response to God's assignment, God will just drop them. There was a young prophet in the book of Kings. God sent him to a place and gave him a specific instruction. "Don't go back the way you came." "Deliver the message. There are people in that time that I can use, but I did not use them. I picked you to do this assignment. "Don't go back the same way you came." That was the instruction.

God said to him, "don't sit down. Don't rest." The young prophet was going and got to a place and sat down to rest. Then the big prophet that was in town that God did not use now showed up. The prophet now says to the young prophet, "I heard you were in town to do some work. Glory be to God." He invites the young prophet to his house to eat. The young prophet decides to follow the prophet home to eat. The young prophet followed the prophet to his house and while the young prophet was eating, the word of God came to the older prophet. God spoke to the older prophet with a message for the young prophet and said "because you have disobeyed me, when you are leaving this place and on your way, a lion will meet you and kill you."

The older prophet was the same prophet that made the young prophet to disobey God. He was now the same prophet that God used to declare His judgement. The disobedience of the prophet resulted in his rejection by God. A prophet cannot lead a church. It's a thin line. I'm not saying that a pastor cannot operate in the prophetic anointing, but if you are called a prophet you do not go and start a church. If you see most people that call themselves a prophet, they don't have a base. They go from church to church preaching the word of God. They don't sit down and say this is my church because the word of God in their mouth is so strong.

So timing is important and the manner of delivery. Look at Exodus chapter 25:1-2:

***[1]And the Lord spake unto Moses, saying, [2]Speak unto the children of Israel, that they bring me an offering: of every man that giveth it willingly with his heart ye shall take my offering***

It's not everything that God tells you, that you say publicly. Like you have a revelation in the service, and I'm greeting people. I am standing with people and you are there, "Pastor, this is what the Lord is saying." That is not the place to tell me what God is saying you wait. When I'm in the way to my office, you can come and meet me  and now tell me what the Lord is saying.

So, maturity comes only in the place of delivery. Can you imagine if Esther would have opened her mouth in front of all of those leaders accusing Haman that he is the one that wanted to kill her people, they would not have listened to her neither the king.

Secondly, she was not truthful about her citizenship. No one knew that Esther was a Jew. She never disclosed it to anybody. That was the instruction that Mordecai gave her. So, if she had said that in front of everybody, all of the leaders would have said to the King, “you married this woman and she is not a part of us. She cannot be a queen”. Death sentence would have been passed immediately.

God’s plan through Esther would have ended badly. Or, it may not have turned out the way that it turned out. Esther would not have found favor the way she found favor with the King if she had said it in front of everybody else.

1. The place of delivery is also important. The wording, the way you word it, is also important. Wording of the message is also important. The intent of your heart while you are delivering the message is also important. If your flesh is involved in delivering that message, you will not deliver it the way God wants you to deliver it. The content must also be of great importance.

So how do you deliver the message? The first thing a prophet should ask the Lord each time He gives you a revelation is how He wants the word to be delivered. I know it's difficult for a prophet to go to a King's house to tell the king that he is going to die. If you look at the way that prophet delivered the message in Isaiah 20. You will see that he uses wisdom. He said prepare your house because this sickness is unto death. He did not say you are going to die. He put all the blame on the sickness. There must be a way of packaging that word. Remember, you are just an instrument. Make sure that you depend on him totally for the delivery of the message.

2. Your responsibility is to deliver the word the way He wants it. You are not accountable to the results for the outcome of the word because it is not your word. If it was your word, then you can be held accountable. Thank God Isaiah had that understanding that the prophet did not come and speak his own word. It was the word of God. That's why he was not treated badly. The king turned to the wall and prayed to the One that sent the word.

If he could get the One that send the word's attention, the message will change. So that's what God did. When he prayed to God the owner of the message, the message change. God told the prophet again as he was going to go back and change the message. Isn't that amazing?

I've heard people tell me that God cannot change his plan. It is a lie. God can change his plan any time. Remember, He is a sovereign God. Nobody can question him.

We don't know how far the prophet had gone, but the Bible says he was in the court. So, he had not gone far. God told him to go back. It's amazing how God can change his plans if you touch his heart. Remember, God has a heart. God told Solomon that his dad was a man after his own heart. "So, if you follow my instructions and do it the way David did, I will favor you just like I favored your dad".

So God has a heart. So, if you can touch his heart then He can change any plan that He originally had made against the nation, again that family, or against that household. So as an instrument you must understand that.

Let's look at another example in Isaiah 41:15.

***15 Behold, I will make thee a new sharp threshing instrument having teeth: thou shalt thresh the mountains, and beat them small, and shalt make the hills as chaff.*** Amen.

You are an instrument. You are nothing in the hand of God but an instrument. No matter the Revelation He has given you, He might decide not to use you anymore. You are just an instrument. He can make you sharp or He can make you dull. He can make you an abandoned instrument or a usable or profitable instrument. He may change his mind totally about you, your family, or your generation. You are just an instrument.

Once you remember that it keeps us humble. It keeps us very humble because without humility you cannot do this work.

3. The Holy Spirit is responsible to get the word to where it is needed. He is an expert at getting the word of one crying in the

wilderness into the King's house. Have you all thought about it? How can John who looks like a madman in the desert get a crowd? It was the Holy Spirit that carried his voice and the people were coming even though he looked so ugly. So you understand what the Holy Spirit can do. He is responsible to carry the voice out. Amen.

He will get the word to where it is needed. This is why when the three Hebrew boys were declaring that they would not worship the idols, God heard them in Heaven and sent His Son to wait for them in the fire. So when they got into the fire, Jesus was already there bringing the temperature down. The temperature was already comfortable even though physically the ones that threw them into the fire died. So you can understand how God works. The Holy Spirit has the potency to deliver the message to wherever you wanted to go. Amen. Therefore speak the Word only.

Let us look at 2 Kings 6:1-4

***1And the sons of the prophets said unto Elisha, Behold now, the place where we dwell with thee is too strait for us. 2Let us go, we pray thee, unto Jordan, and take thence every man a beam, and let us make us a place there, where we may dwell. And he answered, Go ye. 3And one said, Be content, I pray thee, and go with thy servants. And he answered, I will go. 4So he went with them. And when they came to Jordan, they cut down wood.***

That word was spoken and things began to happen. They got favor. They began to borrow axes. Miracles began to happen because of a Word. You think it's easy to just borrow prophet's axes? Someone that is always moving around? How would you borrow the axes to a prophet's son that you may not see you again? Nor has an address? Have you thought about where did the prophet's son get the axe? The moment that Word went out and the man of God agreed to it, things began to happen. So you can see how powerful the Word of God is.

#4. Communicate clearly and precisely. One thing I want all of us to understand is this, when you are delivering the message, allow the Holy Spirit to use you so that the person that you are delivering the message has no doubt as to when, what, and why you are saying what you are saying.

Let me give you a powerful example. Remember Joseph. Remember Joseph was a type of a prophet. Did you know that? When he interpreted that dream to Pharaoh, there was no doubt in Pharaoh's mind that he knew what he was talking about.

So, when they looked for someone to handle that business, they had to choose him because he gave them the clarity of the dream and what was coming. So, there was no doubt in their minds that this boy knows what he is talking about. Not only did he interpret the dream, he told them how to solve the problem. He was clear and precise.

Let us look at another example. Let's look at 2 Kings 5:10

***10 And Elisha sent a messenger unto him, saying, Go and wash in Jordan seven times, and thy flesh shall come again to thee, and thou shalt be clean.***

It was a precise message. It was clear. There was no doubt in the mind of the person receiving the message of what the prophet was saying. It was precise. When God gives instructions like that, it will be clear and precise. If you have a message and the message is not clear or complete, then don't say it. Ask God for the clarity and preciseness of the message.

Sometimes the message will be half clear to the point that you will know the end of the result. Like Jesus Christ told the disciples "go into the city, you will see a man with a pitcher, follow him". It was a message. Clear. Don't follow anybody. Follow the man with the pitcher.

Apparently on that day, because the spirit of God is so powerful, some of you may be asking "Pastor, many men could have had pitchers on that day", but you know God, at that time when Jesus Christ spoke that word, the only pitcher man on site was that man. No other pitcher man. There was no doubt in their mind that man was the pitcher man and that is the one they should follow. It's not that they saw three or four or five and were confused. The message will be precise and clear.

So, when Jesus Christ said follow the pitcher man, by the Spirit of God, He saw in the spirit that by the time they got to that city, the pitcher man that they needed to see would be on the road and they would just connect with him. So there was no doubt.

Even if they saw another pitcher man that day they would not have come out. Are we getting the point? That is how powerful God can work sometimes. God wants us to be clear about what the message is. For example, Jesus Christ told them in the Bible and He prophesied about the walls of Jerusalem and the walls came down just like He said. He prophesied about when and it was precise. So you must know what and about why.

To explain why sometimes might be a little bit tough, let's look at an example in Genesis 41:29-30 to see an example of why. Your communication must be very clear and precise.

***29Behold, there come seven years of great plenty throughout all the land of Egypt: 30And there shall arise after them seven***

***years of famine; and all the plenty shall be forgotten in the land of Egypt; and the famine shall consume the land;***

He gave them precise information. There was no doubt in their mind when it was going to happen. He was telling them when " from now until 7 years, plenty and then after that seven years, seven years of famine". So you must know why.

Sometimes God will give you a message and the when will not be immediate. Let's look at Daniel 5 verses 26 and 28. Sometimes God will give you a message that is not for now but for the future. You must not mix it up. Sometimes God will give you a message and you are thinking that it is going to happen tomorrow, no. That's why we need to ask about how to deliver the message. While you are asking that, God will tell you. Let's look at this example.

***26 This is the interpretation of the thing: Mene; God hath numbered thy kingdom, and finished it. 28 Peres; Thy kingdom is divided, and given to the Medes and Persians.***

He gave a precise and accurate information. There's no doubt in the mind of that King that this man knew what he was talking about. He told him the "why" about the problem. He told him "when", and he told him "what" of the problem. This was not immediately but an interpretation of what was going to happen in the future.

Let's look at another example in Acts 4:36-37.

***36 And Joses, who by the apostles was surnamed Barnabas, (which is, being interpreted, The son of consolation,) a Levite, and of the country of Cyprus, 37 Having land, sold it, and brought the money, and laid it at the apostles' feet.***

This is something very prophetic. It is prophetic because what that man was doing at that time was laying a foundation of the church of the new church age. It was not just these things happening, it was deeper than what we are reading here. These things are not happening today, by the grace of God, today, we see people now not living their lives for Christ because you had to sell everything you have. That's why the judgement of Ananias and Sapphira was so serious because they were not ready to let go of self. That is the basis of the church. That's why the judgement of those people were severe to show us that until we let go of self totally, we cannot enter into the presence of God completely. No flesh. That's why Paul said, "no flesh". So we must understand.

Let us look at another example of prophetic advice. Let us go to Matthew 25. Sometimes your message can be so prophetic that it'll come in the form of advice. Reading from verses 1 and 2.

***[1]Then shall the kingdom of heaven be likened unto ten virgins, which took their lamps, and went forth to meet the bridegroom. [2]And five of them were wise, and five were foolish.***

This parable is an advice to the children of God today that as you walk with Me, you must be prepared for My arrival any time. Jesus Christ was using this parable to let us understand that even today in the body of Christ, we still have people that are foolish thinking that they have all the time to change when they don't have the time.

Can you imagine that these people, the foolish ones, said, "give us some of your oil". The wise ones said, "no we are not giving you our oil". The foolish ones said, "ok, we will quickly run out and buy and then we'll come back". Before they came back, the Master has come. Do you know how many people are playing with their time today?

This kind of parable is an advice to the body of Christ and it's prophetic, and it's a message. It's a message. It's an advice for all the children of God to prepare us that anything can happen at any time if you are not prepared.

It's a message that prepares the children of God as we are walking on this journey, have some extra oil. You never know what's going to happen. Plan your time. Don't overlook any detail. Pray when you are supposed to pray. Don't say, "tonight I am not going to pray, I am tired" because you never know when it is time for the Master to come.

Those people took their assignment with laxity. Why would the other ones take extra oil? Have you ever thought about it? Why? They were serious. They figured out that they did not have an idea of when this bridegroom would come. Since it is late in the night, let us get some extra oil because the people that are selling oil will close and once they close, we can't buy. So, let's buy the extra oil now. So as the day wears on, if the bridegroom does not show up at the time we expect, at least they will have extra oil to put in the lamp. They were prepared. So as a prophet, God can give you a word that will not look like "thus sayeth the Lord" , that will not sound so spiritual, but will still be a very powerful advice for somebody's destiny.

We are going to look at some methods. Now, how do you package the message? Some of the times, the things that confuse us as prophets is that you don't know where you have the lines of the flesh and the spirit. That's why I want us to look at these method. The methods are very, very important.

1. God can use you to speak directly to a person. What do I mean by directly? That means that you just see that person in the store and you say, "ma'am, thus sayeth the Lord". You just speak directly

to that person and even in doing that, time and place have to be seriously considered. If that person was in front of a cashier, the cashier may get in the way. So, you may have to just wait for that person to move from the cashier until that person is on their way to their car to deliver the message. Time and place is still very important. God can use you to speak directly. He does that with a lot of people. The fact that some people can do that it makes them feel as if they are already a prophet which may not be true.

What I mean is that, they do not consider time and place and because they will not give reverence to time and place that anointing becomes an irritation to everybody. They just pull everybody aside. Everywhere they go and it becomes irritating. They don't have anything else to say, but "thus sayeth the Lord". You have to be very careful with that type of anointing. That's why you see those kind of people going up and down prophesying, but they are out of order. We are going to look at the side effects of this.

2. Talking. Sometimes I can be talking to you casually and prophetic word will just come out. That kind of gift is the most overlooked in the prophetic ministry. People don't even take it serious because all they are thinking that you are doing is joking and you are not serious. The word came out as you are talking to them casually and it came from the depth of your spirit and you know that because you know yourself.

You can be talking about a movie and a prophetic word can come from your belly concerning that situation. Most of the time, people overlook that kind of prophetic gift and God uses that a lot. Do you know that's what Jesus Christ used for the woman at the well in Samaria?

He was just talking casually. Jesus said, "how are you today?"

and the woman responded, " I am just here to fetch water." Jesus said, "where do worship?". The woman said, "we don't worship with you anymore, we worship on the mountain." Jesus said, "well, the time is coming where true worshippers will worship God in spirit and in truth". They were not talking spiritual, they were talking casually. However, a word of prophecy came out from the Lord.

Jesus said, "Ok, how was your husband?" The woman said, " Ah, I don't have a husband". (Thank God she told the truth). Casually, but it was prophetic. That kind of gift is the most overlooked especially when you are called to be a prophet by God and He has trained you. You will not be doing it the way other prophets that made themselves prophets. Some people are chosen while others are sent. The chosen one are very real while the sent are many.

Again, I will say to you, some of us God works with our character. A few words that come out of your mouth as an introvert are prophetic, but may not be taken seriously because you did not say, "thus sayeth the Lord". Because that person is operating in his gift, he doesn't talk much naturally. God will still use them under that prophetic ministry and his own gift might be in the style of talking and whatever he says, "Bam!", it works.

That's why when you have that prophetic gift, you have to be really careful what comes out of your mouth. Very, very, very careful. You cannot just talk anyhow. That gift. Take note of that talking gift. Watch people that have that gift. They just talk casually. They won't make a fuss about it. That's just how I feel. That's a lie. It's the word of God coming out of them. Usually, they are very gentle.

Sometimes, God will use a very powerful anointing man who

has walked with the Lord for several years in that prophetic ministry, you will see them operate in all those levels. They can operate as "thus says the Lord" and they can operate as just talking, maybe in counseling you in the office and a prophetic word will just come out during a counseling session. It's still prophetic. If you take hold of that word that they just speak casually, it will work wonders in your life.

I had to make mention of that so that you will watch what you say and listen to yourself. You can also train yourself in that gift. Listen to what comes out of your mouth. Know when it is coming from your well and know when it is coming from your tongue. If it's coming from your well, don't play with it. Write it down. Know that it's prophetic. If it's coming from your tongue, know that you are just talking. You should be able to differentiate between those levels. Amen.

Even though we are prophets, we are still human beings. You still have to be able to relate with your family, but you have to know when and this comes from meditation. You should be able to live a quiet life enough to be able to know the difference of when it is coming from your well and when it is just coming from playing with children.

3. Proxy. Proxy is that God may use a third party to deliver a message. What do I mean by that? Like Jeremiah and Isaiah were like a third party. Jeremiah while he was in prison, he sent Baruck to deliver some messages. He wrote them down. So as a prophetic minister or as an instrument of the Lord, your gifting might be in writing. You might not be able to talk to anybody, but what you write down will go for generations. Nobody will be able to forget you.

So we see Jeremiah was in prison, he was sending people out

to do the work of the ministry. You see Paul, he was in prison. He wrote all those books and we can never forget. He didn't speak to most of those people, it was letters. Letters to the Corinthians. Letters to the Thessalonians. We are still reading them today. Those were powerful prophecies and we see the Word of God come alive. You must understand that God can also use you if you are not able to reach that person. God can use you as an avenue or an individual to help you deliver the message. This is not when the person is accessible or when you just don't like the person. Let's not use that proxy because you don't like the person. Amen. That's why our character must be dwelt with.

As a prophet, you cannot hate nor like that person. You cannot be emotionally involved in the message. You have to do what God tells you to do.

4. Preaching. During normal preaching on Sunday's. During Sunday service, you are preaching, prophetic word will just come out. A prophetic word that comes out during the sermon, most of the time, people miss it. They think you are just preaching, and prophetic words are just coming out. As a church member, you have to pay attention to the Word. Just one word from the mouth of Jehovah can deliver you in just one day. One sentence in a preaching of 20 minutes can change your destiny.

5. Writing. Prophetic word can be in writing. Let's look at Revelation 1:3.

***3Blessed is he that readeth, and they that hear the words of this prophecy, and keep those things which are written therein: for the time is at hand.***

He that read it, so there is a level of reading and a level of writing and preaching. So prophecy can be written down for people to read it and then there are people like me that can read it and then preach it to you.

6. Parable. Prophecy can also be delivered by parable. God can send a man of God to someone to talk about a parable and he is still a prophet. He is just using parable style to deliver the message. Remember, Nathan? Nathan went to David and told him a story. He used that story to draw the emotions of David and when the emotions of David were drawn in it, he told him the truth. Amen.

# CHAPTER 9

# PITFALLS OF THE PROPHETIC MINISTRY

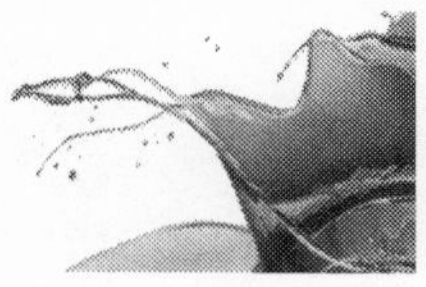

We are going to look at the pitfalls of the prophetic ministry. These are the following areas: areas of influence, areas of money, areas of show off or power, areas of promotion, and in the areas of character. Those are the major areas that the Lord ministered to me about.

We are going to take it one by one and go through the bible to look at examples of what the Lord is saying in those areas. As a prophet, you must understand that your position is very sensitive. It's a thin line. Before you know it, you are already walking in the flesh, and that's why we have to be very careful.

Let's look at the first example, influence. It's easy to get carried away because you have influence and begin to think that you are in charge now and not God anymore. Let's look at 1 Kings 4:21-34. When you are being used again and again by God, most of the time human beings will become very unapproachable thinking that they are so powerful and awesome and no longer submissive to the leading of the Lord, Jesus Christ or the Holy Spirit anymore. Let's read together and see what was the major reason that made Solomon to err.

***21 And Solomon reigned over all kingdoms from the river unto the land of the Philistines, and unto the border of Egypt: they brought presents, and served Solomon all the days of his life.***

22 And Solomon's provision for one day was thirty measures of fine flour, and threescore measures of meal,

23 Ten fat oxen, and twenty oxen out of the pastures, and an hundred sheep, beside harts, and roebucks, and fallowdeer, and fatted fowl. 24 For he had dominion over all the region on this side the river, from Tiphsah even to Azzah, over all the kings on this side the river: and he had peace on all sides round about him.

25 And Judah and Israel dwelt safely, every man under his vine and under his fig tree, from Dan even to Beersheba, all the days of Solomon. 26 And Solomon had forty thousand stalls of horses for his chariots, and twelve thousand horsemen.

27 And those officers provided victual for king Solomon, and for all that came unto king Solomon's table, every man in his month: they lacked nothing. 28 Barley also and straw for the horses and dromedaries brought they unto the place where the officers were, every man according to his charge.

29 And God gave Solomon wisdom and understanding exceeding much, and largeness of heart, even as the sand that is on the sea shore. 30 And Solomon's wisdom excelled the wisdom of all the children of the east country, and all the wisdom of Egypt. 31 For he was wiser than all men; than Ethan the Ezrahite, and Heman, and Chalcol, and Darda, the sons of Mahol: and his fame was in all nations round about. 32 And he spake three thousand proverbs: and his songs were a thousand and five. 33 And he spake of trees, from the cedar

***tree that is in Lebanon even unto the hyssop that springeth out of the wall: he spake also of beasts, and of fowl, and of creeping things, and of fishes.***

***[34] And there came of all people to hear the wisdom of Solomon, from all kings of the earth, which had heard of his wisdom.***

Wow! What an influence. When you have that type of influence, you tend to forget who God is again despite the fact that he was commanded by God to keep His commandments when the Lord came to him in a dream. Remember God appeared to him in a dream and said to him, "keep my commandments just like your father did", but Solomon ended up strange, getting married to thousands of concubines from every nation. He has many wives and that is the beginning of his fall.

You know when you get to a certain level of where God is using you, you prophecy and it came to pass, you speak and it came to pass, you speak into people's lives and you see results, and you are seeing results constantly, you become arrogant. This is what influence can do and that is why we have to talk about it as children of God and as a prophetic minister. Matter of fact, the best thing to do is to go down more and to humble yourself the more. Don't let whatever God is doing through you make you feel as if you are more than Him. There are predecessors ahead of you and there are people coming behind you that are looking up to you. You have to be very careful. There is nothing that any man can do that God has not done before. God is the One that uses us. So the moment you know that it is God using you, He can use you more than the person that anoints you. I may be teaching all of you today, but tomorrow you will be doing things that I have never done.

So, that doesn't mean that your father does not know what he is doing. Amen. The wisdom of the father is the wisdom of the father. So no matter the influence that we have, God warned Solomon, "make sure you keep to My commandments". Look at the influence we just read. How many people would have that type of influence and it will not get to their head? Look at the influence. All over the world, he is known. Look at the things he possess. Look at the land. Look at the properties. Look at the people working under him. It takes extra humility to control that kind of grace.

That is why I had to use that type of example for you. Most of the examples that I use they are basically physical, but you can imagine when you yield that type of influence over destinies. You speak, it comes to pass. You begin to feel like you are the one. No, because the moment that God sees that you are doing like that, the gift of God is without repentance and things will still be happening, but He will never use you again. Now you begin to do it in your effort. It may still work, but it may not work for a long time and God is no longer in it.

So, we have to be careful about our influence because what you carry, you carry the Word. The Word of God does not lie. The Word of God is real. The Word of God performs. The Word of God is a performer. So, when you see the Word of God performing through your mouth again and again, you tend to see your influence expanding. You need to humble yourself. That is the time to humble yourself. God will continue to use you, but don't forget your beginning. That's one thing that Solomon forgot. It was God that brought him to that point. It was God that chose him. It was God that gave him that influence. It was God that made sure that all of his enemies were at peace with him. It wasn't Solomon, it was God. That's why the Bible says, "And God gave

Solomon". It was not his own wisdom, it was God that gave it to him. You want to be really careful about that.

Most of the time when a prophet gets to that point, most prophets don't even know. They don't even know that they are walking in the flesh. They are gifted. They are anointed by God. They are no longer aware that God is no longer in the picture except for the ones who are very sensitive and humble. They have not stopped their prayer life. You know you can get so close to God and enjoy His presence and enjoy the anointing so much that you no longer give yourself to study any more.

You know some pastors are like that? They have notes. That is why I keep on having notes because I don't just go into my archives and pick something out of there and use it to teach. I still have messages that I preached in 2006 and 2005. I still have it on paper in the original handwriting in my file. Any time I want to minister, I will still have to study. I will still have to pray.

The moment we get to a point where we don't have to study anymore or pray because God has used you again and again and you think you know it all and you don't have to wait on the Lord or seek the face of God, it is dangerous. I want you to understand that the Word will still come but it's not from God. It's from you. It's from your archives and not from the Holy Spirit.

Your archives are loaded because God has used you again and again. So, even in your archives, there are some word there that look so powerful, but it's not from God. So, when you have so much influence, you have to be careful.

That's one thing about God that I have discovered is when a baby is growing, like a born again Christian who has just given their life to Christ, the first 2 or 3 years, before you pray, God will answer. Before you scream, God is there. As you mature, He will not be giving you everything you ask for anymore. He's now going to be teaching you how to wait on Him. He will be teaching you how to trust Him. When you don't have, you can still trust Him. He wants you to mature.

Just like a baby in a crib, at first cry, you give them food, right? A time will come when that baby will ask for food when he is hungry. If they don't ask for food, you are not going to give them. That's the same thing about the Kingdom of God, as we mature as a prophet. First of all, when you start as a prophet, walking on that journey, God will be doing many things before you speak, it will happen. You just see miracle here and there. All God is doing is testing you to see whether you will still remain humble or not. As you mature, He will begin to withdraw that privilege. Now, when you speak to people, they will be angry at you.

God now wants to begin to work on your character. "ok, what are you going to do when they don't receive you?" "What are going to do when your word does not come to pass?" "Are you going to be angry at me?" So, He will begin to train you in those areas.

Now, let's talk about money. Money, the Bible says, is the root of all evil. Money is a terrible thing. A lot of people are living under the bondage of money and they don't even know it. When it comes to money, they will scheme and do anything to get it. We must be very careful as a prophet especially when God gives you very highly placed people. You must not try to use your anointing to manipulate them. Amen. You must not because they believe everything you say. They believe every word that comes out of your mouth. Now, when you have that type of idol in your heart or any form of idol, it's very dangerous as a prophet. As a prophet, when you have any idol in your heart, it works silently, it may be an idol of anger, it may be an idol of pride, or it may be an idol of money. If there's any type of idol, it's very dangerous because God sees your heart. Let's look at a powerful example in Ezekiel 14:1-3.

***1Then came certain of the elders of Israel unto me, and sat before me. 2 And the word of the Lord came unto me, saying, 3Son of man, these men have set up their idols in their heart, and put the stumbling block of their iniquity before their face: should I be enquired of at all by them?***

God says these people have already made up their mind about some things in their lives. Those things that are before them, no matter what I say to them, it's not going to change the way they look at things. Why are they coming to me? God says, these ones, they will not listen to what I have to say.

Look at what God says in verse 4.

***4 Therefore speak unto them, and say unto them, Thus saith the Lord GOD; Every man of the house of Israel that setteth up his idols in his heart, and putteth the stumblingblock of his iniquity before his face, and cometh to the prophet; I the LORD will answer him that cometh according to the multitude of his idols;***

Wow! Is that not strange? God says, if you like money, I'm going to talk to you in the area of your money so you will feel good about where you are going. Just like Jesus Christ told Judas, "whatever you are going to do. I see that you love money. You want to go and betray me. That's good, you will not hear. Whatever you are going to do, do it quickly."

So, God can work in two ways. Just like He interceded on behalf of Peter even though both of them had betrayed Him, but the heart of Peter was pure. The heart of Judas, he had an idol there. It is money. He loves money, and God knows that this idol in the heart of Judas will not deliver him. So, "whatever you want to go and do, quickly, go and do it".

While He was praying for the other one to be delivered from the betrayal, He was telling the other one, "quickly whatever you have to do, go and do it". So, you have to be very careful about idols in our hearts.

Let's look at Acts 8:14-20.

***14 Now when the apostles which were at Jerusalem heard that Samaria had received the word of God, they sent unto them Peter and John: 15 Who, when they were come down, prayed for them, that they might receive the Holy Ghost:***

***16 (For as yet he was fallen upon none of them: only they were baptized in the name of the Lord Jesus.) 17 Then laid they their hands on them, and they received the Holy Ghost. 18 And when Simon saw that through laying on of the apostles' hands the Holy Ghost was given, he offered them money,***
***19 Saying, Give me also this power, that on whomsoever I lay hands, he may receive the Holy Ghost. 20 But Peter said unto him, Thy money perish with thee, because thou hast thought that the gift of God may be purchased with money.***

Now, where this story is so important is that thank God Peter and John did not like money. If they loved money, they would have settled for that arrangement. Peter and John are broke, they are prophets. Those men would have given Peter and John money to get that power too. That's why money is very dangerous for someone that carries anointing because at every point and time in your life, you will be tempted with money either personally (not from outside when you are supposed to give money but you don't want to give because you are thinking about your future, your life, and you refuse to give that money) or it may be from outside to test your position on money issues.

Peter and John were tested on money issues and anybody that does not know the God they are serving would have settled for that. "Let's give you some money. This power you have, maybe we can use it too." That's why it's dangerous. When you carry anointing like that, when you meet with great people with money, they may try to manipulate you because they have money. You should not settle for that. My ten cents with peace is better than one dollar with trouble. I don't need your dollar. If I don't have money, I prefer it than to give away my destiny because of money.

This God that we are serving, many people don't even know Him. He reserves the right to do things the way He likes to do them. He reserves the power. He reserves the sovereign right to choose the way He will build His church. He reserves the right to use you the way He likes. Tell me the truth, if God speak to Joel Osteen to leave that 16,000 or 30,000 membership to go and start from scratch in another location, how many people would answer that type of call? How many pastors would answer that call?

First of all, they will say that it is the devil. To leave all that was done to go and start from scratch again? God reserves the right. He can say or give that instruction to any pastor because we are an instrument and it is not our property. God says, He will build His church, it is not our church. He reserves the right to give you instructions any way He chooses. He reserves the right to use you any way He likes. Since the brother opened the eyes of Saul who changed his name to Paul, did we hear his name again? Did you hear anything about that brother again?

So, we must understand this God and the way He operates. Some people think that because we are in the millennial age, in the 21st century, God cannot do those things anymore. Who told you that when the Bible clearly tells us in Hebrew that He is the same yesterday, today, and forever.

He can do anything He chooses to do. When the tsunami struck in 2004, do you know how many people perished? Was there a thunder in Heaven? Were there angels everywhere to mourn the dead? Was there a colossal mourning from Heaven and we see the tears from God coming from Heaven to weep over the ones that died? No, that nation was full of idols and they were judged. God allowed that to happen. No evil can happen without God's permission. When He refers to snow as a messenger, (the treasure of snow) and floods are clapping for Him, what is that thing that can move without His knowledge?

Nothing moves without His permission. If anything perishes, if anything dies, He has an idea of what's going on. Nothing is new to Him. Nothing is new to Him about what you are doing now. Nothing is new to Him about what is in your heart. Nothing is new to Him about what you are going through. It may be new to you, but it is not new to Him. So, we must understand this God.

When we have idol in our heart, it is a dangerous thing as a prophet because you won't be able to function very well. You will function haphazardly. That is why the judgement of lukewarm people is very severe. The Bible says that God will spew you out.

So, this journey that we are walking is of total obedience. Don't let anybody draw you into any iniquity because people will offer you money. They will offer you things. They will offer you fame. They will offer you influence. Don't let anybody put you in that spot because number one, they are not going to where you are going and number two, they will drag you down in to their iniquity. So, we must be very careful. Thank God it was Peter and John and not Judas. Judas would have taken the money.

Let's look at another example of this money issue in Numbers 22:1-7

***1 And the children of Israel set forward, and pitched in the plains of Moab on this side Jordan by Jericho. 2 And Balak the son of Zippor saw all that Israel had done to the Amorites. 3 And Moab was sore afraid of the people, because they were many: and Moab was distressed because of the children of Israel.***

***4 And Moab said unto the elders of Midian, Now shall this company lick up all that are round about us, as the ox licketh up the grass of the field. And Balak the son of Zippor was king of the Moabites at that time. 5 He sent messengers therefore unto Balaam the son of Beor to Pethor, which is by the river of the land of the children of his people, to call him, saying, Behold, there is a people come out from Egypt: behold, they cover the face of the earth, and they abide over against me:***

***6 Come now therefore, I pray thee, curse me this people; for they are too mighty for me: peradventure I shall prevail, that we may smite them, and that I may drive them out of the land: for I wot that he whom thou blessest is blessed, and he***

***whom thou cursest is cursed. [7] And the elders of Moab and the elders of Midian departed with the rewards of divination in their hand; and they came unto Balaam, and spake unto him the words of Balak.***

Did you read that? Rewards of divination. If people that are unbelievers know how to sow seed to men of God for their labor, I don't know why church can't do that. These are unbelievers that are not going empty handed. They are going with something.

Let's continue verse 8.

***[8] And he said unto them, Lodge here this night, and I will bring you word again, as the LORD shall speak unto me: and the princes of Moab abode with Balaam.***

At this point, Balaam was fantastic. He saw all the money they brought and said that he was not going to tell them anything until he sleeps over it and talks with God overnight to see what the Lord has to say.

Let's continue verse 9-12

***[9] And God came unto Balaam, and said, What men are these with thee? [10] And Balaam said unto God, Balak the son of Zippor, king of Moab, hath sent unto me, saying, [11] Behold, there is a people come out of Egypt, which covereth the face of the earth: come now, curse me them; peradventure I shall be able to overcome them, and drive them out. [12] And God said unto Balaam, Thou shalt not go with them; thou shalt not curse the people: for they are blessed.***

Is that not enough for any man of God to back off from that

assignment? Because there was an idol in the heart of Balaam, he saw all the money that they brought, he thought that he had to get something.

Let's continue verse 13-14

***[13] And Balaam rose up in the morning, and said unto the princes of Balak, Get you into your land: for the LORD refuseth to give me leave to go with you. [14] And the princes of Moab rose up, and they went unto Balak, and said, Balaam refuseth to come with us.***

That is very fantastic. He did well.

Next verse, verses 15-16.

***[15] And Balak sent yet again princes, more, and more honourable than they.[16] And they came to Balaam, and said to him, Thus saith Balak the son of Zippor, Let nothing, I pray thee, hinder thee from coming unto me:***

That means anything he wanted, any money that he needed. That means if they did not bring enough money when they came, when he would come, they would have more. They told Balaam not to let anything stand in his way.

Next verse, verse 17.

***[17] For I will promote thee unto very great honour, and I will do whatsoever thou sayest unto me: come therefore, I pray thee, curse me this people.***

People will offer you to go places that you have never been. It's good to hear those things. When people say those things to you, it makes you feel good, but in the future, they are going to back away from you when God begins to deal with you.

Verse 18

***[18] And Balaam answered and said unto the servants of Balak, If Balak would give me his house full of silver and gold, I cannot go beyond the word of the LORD my God, to do less or more.***

That is still a good answer, but look at what he says next in verse 19.

***[19] Now therefore, I pray you, tarry ye also here this night, that I may know what the LORD will say unto me more.***

He has finished himself. Why would he tell them to tarry? "Let me check again with the Lord?" "Maybe He will change His mind." The Lord has spoken the first time. He has said that these people are blessed, and you cannot curse this ones. Why is Balaam telling them to tarry? There is an idol somewhere.

He saw all that money and said, "God, you have to change your mind". "Let me be blessed by these people. You know I am a poor man." "The King needs my attention." "God, please change your mind."

Let's look at what God says. Let's read verse 20.

***[20] And God came unto Balaam at night, and said unto him, If the men come to call thee, rise up, and go with them; but yet the word which I shall say unto thee, that shalt thou do.***

Do you know why God had to agree with him? Why go back to God when He has already spoken? When God sees an idol in your heart, He will not want to give up on change, but God will go with you because He wants to destroy it. He will go with your plan. He will go with your agenda. He will go with the fun fare. He will go with everything you are planning in your heart because He wants to destroy it. Can you imagine God is the One telling him to go.

Let's see what happens in verse 21-22.

***21 And Balaam rose up in the morning, and saddled his ass, and went with the princes of Moab. 22 And God's anger was kindled because he went: and the angel of the LORD stood in the way for an adversary against him. Now he was riding upon his ass, and his two servants were with him.***

Can you imagine if God is the One that is really telling him from His heart to go, why is He angry with him? It is because the man of God will not stop asking Him the same question. God has told him "no" the first time He spoke, but because of what Balaam wants to eat, the promotion, and accolades and God knows that Balaam likes them.

So, if Balaam wants to go, God lets him go. Even though, God tells him to go, God is still angry with him. That is why prophets must be very careful. God can tell you to do this thing and now you are changing your mind because people and what they are saying and the money and influence. God will go with you and your plan and His plan is to destroy it.

Look at what happened in the next few verses. Starting at verse 23.

***23 And the ass saw the angel of the LORD standing in the way, and his sword drawn in his hand: and the ass turned aside out of the way, and went into the field: and Balaam***

***smote the ass, to turn her into the way.***

If God wanted to kill him, He told the angel to go and stand in his way because this man will not hear. When I show him, he will understand. In God's infinite mercy, the donkey that Balaam was riding saw the angel with the sword to kill this man of God. This donkey would not move forward. This man was kicking the donkey. The donkey had to speak. This is to let you know that when you have idols, you can't hear again.

You cannot hear. You cannot see because you are enjoying the fun fare. You are enjoying the money. You are enjoying the accolades. So, you cannot hear anything anymore because your eyes and your mind are totally blocked. Can you imagine a man of God, a prophet did not even see the angel? It was the animal. That lets you know that the anointing was gone totally. At this point, he is totally in the flesh. He could not hear. He could not see the angel. He could not sense in the spirit that God was not pleased with him.

You know when you are in the flesh, you cannot please God. When you are in the flesh, you cannot even sense when God is pleased with you or not. You cannot because your mind is totally on the money.

Only God knows what He was planning to do once he got the money. Because this man was totally in the flesh, he does not know whether he is pleasing God anymore. That's why it's dangerous for a prophet to be in the flesh because you will miss God.

Please, I beg of you don't mix the anointing with money at all. Maybe that's one of the reasons that the Lord has preserved me. Something happened to me, my wife is my witness, a family I was praying with asked me to start the ministry at another location.

They promised to support me with anything. I told them that I knew their Pastor very well and that he was my friend. I would not stab him in the back. I went on to say that if anything at all and God tells you to support the ministry, go and pray. If God tells you that, then go and tell your Pastor what the Lord is saying that they should join the ministry under me. Let the Pastor pray for the family and then release them. I told them, anything short of that, I would not do it.

I prefer not to do that. Stay in your church and grow there, except the Lord tells you, then go and tell your Pastor. Make sure that you are released. To tell you the truth, none of them has come back. That's why you have to be careful with people. Most people will push you to do what you don't plan to do. As a child of God, as a true prophet of God, you must draw the line.

I want to stand before Jesus and say "Lord, I did everything you asked me to do." Even if people don't love me or respect me, I don't care. I want to stand in the place of the truth. It doesn't matter. I want to be able to look at Jesus and say, "I did my best." I'm not the first person that they would hate. They hated Jesus. They even called Him devil. Somebody that is so righteous. They told Him that His father was the devil. They have not said that to me.

So, you must be able to stand in the place of righteousness. Don't compromise. You see Balaam here. Does God change His words like that when God told him from the get-go, "do not go with them". "These people are blessed." What else does he want to hear? God spared his life. God does not give everyone that type of opportunity to redeem yourself. Some people do die in their disobedience.

Another point is power. Power can make us to believe that it is all you. It will make you to show off to say that "if it was not for you". You need to thank God that God is using you. Amen. Praise the Lord.

One thing that God has given me grace for is that I can never be intimidated by someone else's success because my desire is to see others do great things. If anyone of you begins to raise the dead, I will be happy. Whatever it is that you have done, God has used me to pour something inside of you. So whatever you are doing, you are sons and daughters of the ministry of where you are.

So, when you have power to the point that you do not know your source anymore, oh my goodness, it is very dangerous. Let's look at brother Samson because he's a good example. Let's look at the book of Judges and see what Brother Samson did.

Let's look at Judges 14:1-2.

***1And Samson went down to Timnath, and saw a woman in Timnath of the daughters of the Philistines. 2 And he came up, and told his father and his mother, and said, I have seen a woman in Timnath of the daughters of the Philistines: now therefore get her for me to wife.***

That is very good. He came back to his parents.

Now in verse 3.

***3 Then his father and his mother said unto him, Is there never a woman among the daughters of thy brethren, or among all my people, that thou goest to take a wife of the uncircumcised Philistines? And Samson said unto his father, Get her for me; for she pleaseth me well.***

When did that start where your father cannot talk to you? Now that you are anointed, your father cannot talk to you again? So people of God, no matter what God is using you to do, if the Holy Spirit tells you to keep quiet and don't talk, even if you have the revelation of the whole world in your mouth, keep quiet. Even if God has been using you time and time and time again. Everything you do is accurate, everything you do is powerful, if the Holy Spirit says to keep quiet, keep quiet.

The Holy Spirit will speak to you and it is up to you to listen. He will not shut your mouth. You must control yourself. It is His work. No matter how you feel. You may not like it, but it is His work.

Can you imagine? Samson's father spoke in some very strong words concerning this Philistine woman and yet Samson would not listen. That was the beginning of his downfall. Once there is an idol in your heart, God will approve what you are doing, but you will kill yourself.

You think God really planned for Samson to die the way he died? Once we have chosen our paths and not listen anymore, the anointing will still be there to do small things, but your eyes will be pulled out.

If God has mercy on you, the anointing will grow back again so you can kill some more people before you die too. It doesn't happen like that all the time. God had to show Samson mercy. Samson had to cry out unto the Lord. He made his hair to grow and God gave him grace to kill more people at the end. So that doesn't mean we should do that type of walk that Samson walked. That walk was a wicked walk. It was a walk of destruction. It was a walk that destroyed him totally.

There are some Delilah's in your life now that you have to be careful. Delilah can be in the form of your character, money, disobedience spirit that is always pushing you to not listen to your Pastor. You know God does not always give this type of privilege so it is a joy for me to teach this. I honor you so much. If God makes you to be great, I will be so glad.

Samson forgot his root. He forgot who he was. He forgot his beginning. He forgot what made him to be what he is. He forgot that there was a father and a mother that the angel appeared to bring him to life. He forgot that his daddy, even though his daddy does not exercise the power that he has, was still his father. No matter what you achieve in life, humble yourself. Before destruction is pride. Humble yourself.

If you will not humble yourself to people that launch you out to make you what you are, you will finish yourself. Samson would not listen to his parents because now he thinks he has anointing. That was his down spiral for his destruction. You think God would want someone to mess with His anointed one like that? Pull out his eyes? Making him to be crying out. You think that was the plan of God for the man of God? When He can protect Nebuchadnezzar? When He can protect David in his sin? No one overthrew David. He can protect Nebuchadnezzar in his failure. His throne was vacant for seven years and no one dared to go there. God protects his people except you are not willing to humble yourself.

When you are not willing to be humble. When you are not willing to be broken, that's when God exposes you. With all humility, I am sharing this. Even when Saul was messing up, He would not let David touch him.

So, when somebody is in sin and God does not allow his

contemporary to touch him, then do you think He would allow the members of the church or world to touch him? When you are not broken that's why God oversees the judgement of Saul. They killed him and his children. They made sure that there was no competition against David's throne. Saul and his family was completely destroyed. He only spared Mephibosheth because of the covenant between David and Jonathan. That was it.

God made sure even the one that was spared was paralyzed and could not fight any battle. He was at the mercy of David. God made sure that He completely finished that generation. This is God we are talking about. How many times did Saul repent? If Saul would have truly repented and humbled himself, you think God would have allowed him to die the way he was killed? God does not punish His anointed ones the way He punishes anybody on the street. He will protect you. He will talk to you. He will try to change you while you are under the anointing. Aaron did not die until he removed the priestly garment even though he misbehaved like Miriam, God did not punish him. God punished Miriam. God was waiting for the right time, the moment he removed the priestly garment, God killed him immediately. The anointing protects you.

That's why some people think they can mess up and do anything because they carry anointing. One has to be very careful with this anointing. Samson misbehaved big time and God was not happy with him. How would God allow some people to remove His anointed one's eyes? Do you know what that means? You think God is happy? When you live recklessly outside of the will of God, that's what happens. May the Lord help us in the name of Jesus. Amen.

Now, let's talk about promotion. You know with your anointing, your gift will make room for you. With the anointing, people will be giving you attention and all these things. You will be promoted. You will be moving up in the hierarchy. You are now prophesying to the city and now you are talking to the president. As you are moving up like that, you have to be really careful and remain genuine and humble. Once you do not, you are setting yourself up for failure.

Let's look at an example in Matthew 20:20-28.

***[20]Then came to him the mother of Zebedees children with her sons, worshipping him, and desiring a certain thing of him. [21]And he said unto her, What wilt thou? She saith unto him, Grant that these my two sons may sit, the one on thy right hand, and the other on the left, in thy kingdom. [22]But Jesus answered and said, Ye know not what ye ask. Are ye able to drink of the cup that I shall drink of, and to be baptized with the baptism that I am baptized with? They say unto him, We are able. [23]And he saith unto them, Ye shall drink indeed of my cup, and be baptized with the baptism that I am baptized with: but to sit on my right hand, and on my left, is not mine to give, but it shall be given to them for whom it is prepared of my Father. [24]And when the ten heard it, they were moved with indignation against the two brethren. [25]But Jesus called them unto him, and said, Ye know that the princes of the Gentiles exercise dominion over them, and they that are great exercise authority upon them. [26]But it shall not be so among you: but whosoever will be great among you, let him be your minister; [27]And whosoever will be chief among you, let him be your servant:28 Even as the Son of man came not to be ministered unto, but to minister, and to give his life a ransom for many.***

I love Jesus. First of all, He blesses them with problems. Then

He tells them that the promotion that they are looking for, it is not for Him to give. I love Jesus. They are not even in the number while the others were angry not even knowing what Jesus was saying to the two. That's why you should not be angry when you see someone always in your Pastor's office. Do you know why the Pastor is calling them in? Can you do what the person being called can do? If your Pastor was to give you the assignments that he is giving to the person in his office, will you do it? Don't be jealous of something you don't know the details about. Angry for what? Are you ready to die on the cross or do you need your own cup of suffering? You see how people are? They want to be like you. They want to be like the Pastor.

So, Jesus says, you want to be great, let others walk over you. You want to sit on my left and my right hand? Serve people. Let them insult you. Let them spit on you. Nobody want to go through that. People want to be leaders, but they don't want to serve. Praise the Lord.

We must be very careful, amen. If the Lord is using you on the level of individual, don't just jump to the next level. There is a sacrifice to be paid. May the Lord help us in the name of Jesus. Amen.

Let's look at character. One thing I want us to look at in character is that it requires 200% self-control. As a prophet, as a prophetic minister, you must exercise absolute self-control. You must not do things out of feelings. You must not do things out of emotions. You must not do things out of the way you feel about it because your judgement may be very wrong in the sight of God. You might use that anointing in a very wrong way. The Lord will help us in the name of Jesus. Amen.

Let us look at this powerful example that the Lord gave to me. 2

Kings 2:23-24.

***[23] And he went up from thence unto Bethel: and as he was going up by the way, there came forth little children out of the city, and mocked him, and said unto him, Go up, thou bald head; go up, thou bald head. [24] And he turned back, and looked on them, and cursed them in the name of the LORD. And there came forth two she bears out of the wood, and tare forty and two children of them.***

Can you believe that? You have to be very careful what you do with the anointing. We know that those children did not have any home training. This training is to teach you so that when you carry yourself to another church somewhere and the Lord uses you there, you just don't become too highly exalted. Remember, you are just an instrument.

I know why God did that. He wanted to train Elijah. Remember, the anointing was fresh. He just did a fantastic job of healing the waters of Jericho. That's why you have to be very careful with power. So he was going with that type of power of anyone that would mess with him, he would deal with them. Elijah has just taken care of a problem that Joshua cursed several years ago. He was going with that arrogance and the test came about his character from children, and he reacted and he was finished. One thing about it is that, the water will still come out even though you misbehaved. The water still came out when Moses disobeyed because God was thinking about the people that were thirsty. God still allowed that to happen just like He allowed Balaam. As a representative of God, sometimes the things you do in the flesh, God will still honor it, but that doesn't mean that God likes it. That's why we have to be careful. My prayers is that we will not become an abandoned instrument in the hand of God because of a character flaw in our lives. May God have mercy. In Jesus Name. Amen.

# NOTES

Made in the USA
Middletown, DE
09 January 2022